THE FLIGH

FOR MICHAEL PICARD

Quo ibit fugiturus iste a facie Dei? Vertit se hac atque illac, quasi quaerens locum fugae suae . . . Quo iturus es, quo fugies? Si vis ab illo fugere, ad ipsum fuge. Ad ipsum fuge confitendo, non ab ipso latendo: latere enim non potes, sed confiteri potes.

St. Augustine

THE HUMANIST LIBRARY

The FLIGHT from GOD

MAX PICARD

With a Note on MAX PICARD
by GABRIEL MARCEL
and an Introduction
by J. M. CAMERON

Translated from the German by
MARIANNE KUSCHNITZKY and
J.M. CAMERON

REGNERY GATEWAY
Washington, D.C.

First published by Eugen Rentsch Verlag, Erlenbach,
Switzerland, 1934
First Regnery Gateway, Inc. printing, 1951

Library of Congress Cataloging-in-Publication Data

Picard, Max. 1888–1965.
  [Flucht von Gott. English]
  The flight from God / Max Picard ; with a note on
Max Picard by Gabriel Marcel and an introduction by
J.M. Cameron ; translated from the German by Marianne
Kuschnitzky and J.M. Cameron.
      p.   cm.
  Translation of: Flucht von Gott.
  ISBN 0-89526-752-7   (alk. paper)
  1. Apostasy. 2. Secularism. I. Title.
BL2747.P53   1989
233—dc20   89-38837
                                                   CIP

Published in the United States by
Regnery Gateway
1130 17th Street, NW
Washington, DC 20036

Distributed to the trade by
National Book Network
4720-A Boston Way
Lanham, MD 20706

1989 printing
Printed on acid free paper
Manufactured in the United States of America

CONTENTS

	PAGE
TRANSLATORS' NOTE	vi
MAX PICARD, Note by GABRIEL MARCEL	vii
INTRODUCTION by J. M. CAMERON	xv
DESCRIPTION OF THE FLIGHT	1
THE CONSTRUCTION OF THE FLIGHT	10
THE ORGANIZATION OF THE FLIGHT	25
DESOLATION IN THE FLIGHT	57
DREAD IN THE FLIGHT	68
THE IMITATION OF GOD IN THE FLIGHT	79
ECONOMICS IN THE WORLD OF THE FLIGHT	91
LANGUAGE IN THE WORLD OF FAITH AND IN THE WORLD OF THE FLIGHT	102
THINGS IN THE WORLD OF THE FLIGHT	126
ART IN THE WORLD OF THE FLIGHT	138
THE IMAGE AND THE FLIGHT	148
THE FACE OF MAN IN THE FLIGHT	159
THE GREAT CITY AND NATURE IN THE FLIGHT	170
THE PURSUER	181

ACKNOWLEDGMENTS

Our thanks are due to Messrs P. V. and A. E. Dobell for permission to quote from Traherne's "Centuries of Meditations," page 112, and to Messrs John Lane, The Bodley Head, for the quotation from James Joyce's "Ulysses" on pages 112 and 113.

TRANSLATORS' NOTE

It is not possible to give a fully satisfactory rendering of Dr. Picard's vigorous and highly idiosyncratic German. Where it has seemed to us of first importance to convey Dr. Picard's meaning we have not hesitated—if there seemed to us no other possibility—to err on the side of literalness and to offer a version which reads like a translation. Where we have judged the point of a passage to lie rather in its poetic power than in its literal meaning we have attempted, with, we fear, very imperfect success, to give something of an *equivalent*, without altogether leaving translation for paraphrase.

M. K.

J. M. C.

MAX PICARD

PICARD was born in 1888 at Schopfheim in the
Grand Duchy of Baden. His parents were Swiss,
of Jewish origin, but Picard himself is a convert to
Roman Catholicism. His first intention was to
become a doctor and he completed his medical
studies in Germany. It is said that he had a great
talent for diagnosis, which is not surprising, for he is a
born physician. Soon, however, the mechanical
methods of therapy then in use disgusted him and he
abandoned medicine for the study of philosophy,
which he pursued at Heidelberg.

After his marriage he settled in the Ticino in
Switzerland on account of his wife's health and has
for many years lived on the banks of the Lake of
Lugano, a few miles from the Italian frontier. His
writings comprise several published works and a
number of MSS which he intends to print when the
time seems appropriate to him.

This is as much as needs to be known about the
facts of the author's life.

Max Picard is a "sage". He is not at all a philosopher if by philosopher we mean a professor of philosophy. But then perhaps Nietzsche showed a prophetic insight when he denounced all professors of philosophy after Schopenhauer. Perhaps it is true that it is less and less possible for philosophy to be taught from a rostrum. Professors are always in danger of subtly betraying the very ideas they have undertaken to disseminate, and it may yet prove to be the chief merit of existential philosophy that it has made this danger clear and that it has thrown light upon the "philosophic life".

Picard is one of the few Westerners who gives us a convincing example of this "philosophic existence". The reason for this is that he has retained the sense of contemplation in a high degree. For him contemplation is not merely something for which he feels a need, it enters into his life and is part of his being. That is why it is so difficult to think of him apart from the surroundings in which he lives and has taken root, though this is the more curious since he is not a native of the Ticino but has adopted it— or perhaps we might say (it comes to the same thing) that he has been adopted by this good land in which grandeur and intimacy are united.

I think that, fully to understand his work, it is necessary not only to have seen his life but also to have lived it, at least for a few days. It will then become apparent that what I have said of the Ticino is true also of him. A small man, he is yet informed with a certain majesty. Unfortunately this word nowadays suggests some kind of pretentiousness or bogus solemnity ; nothing could be further from Picard's personality. Majesty in him is allied to a complete simplicity, I would even say to an irreducible humility. Though here again we must define our words, for now, when we speak of humility, we usually have in mind a false humility, a particularly disagreeable trait since it is contrary to the essential dignity of the human being; and it is just this quality of dignity (rendered by the German word *würde*) which is characteristic of Picard. Perhaps we might say that his dignity is that of one who knows himself to be a creature of God and who also knows himself as un- alterably bound to his Creator.

Taking "religion" in its etymological sense of "bond" or "relation" (the *religacion* on which the Spanish philosopher Zubiri insists so strongly) we could say that it is because Picard is a religious man that he is always in communication with simple people, real people, and that he has a horror of pretentiousness. This trait also shows itself in his piety toward food, necessary food, bread particularly; this piety is very near to the Gospels. Never, I think,

have I met a person who seemed to me so true
and also so hungry for truth. If, for instance, he
is pitiless in speaking of certain contemporary
thinkers and writers (mostly German ones, though
German is his own tongue), it is because, with an
almost infallible intuition, he senses in them something hollow—the presence of a lie. And if he has
a horror of Zürich and sometimes talks of it as an
accursed town, it is because he sees it as one of the
capitals of that hollow modern world which he
condemns, as did Péguy, whom he loves and understands so well.

I have had the privilege of spending a few days
with this astonishing man. Never have I met anyone
less academic, less ready to conform to a con-
ventional type. He is spontaneity and life itself;
this shows itself even in his features, with their un-
believable mobility and at times mocking expression.
His opinions, which are often severe, always seem
to come from an incontrovertible basis, and with
this basis I felt in direct communication, even though
I was sometimes disconcerted by the vehemence of
his opinions. I told him, which seemed to surprise
him, that, seeing him live his life, I was reminded of
some English eighteenth-century personage, a Tom
Jones for instance. But what a change took place
whenever our conversation touched the level of con-

templation, the visionary plane which is always present in his work.

It would be quite impossible, I think, to attribute anything like a system to him. With him, intuition is everything, or more precisely "fulguration" is everything. Nothing could be more characteristic of this than his method of making his books. He always advances by short chapters, each corresponding to a certain aspect of the fundamental subject just as though he were travelling round it in a circle and surveying the whole of it from every successive viewpoint. "Aspect", "view-point", would have to be given a fuller meaning than is current to explain this process. Picard's imagination is essentially plastic, and indeed, his whole metaphysics of "countenance" (which involves much more than the physical contour of the "face") is only conceivable in these terms.

In *The Flight from God* Picard gives us the key to his thought. The whole of our world, as opposed to the abolished world of faith, is in flight. No longer does anyone ask before whom he flees, or why he flees; no one remembers that he flees from God. Flight has taken to itself a sort of independent existence; it has become an entity.

The originality of Picard's intuition, I would almost say his genius, lies in having discovered that the Flight has assumed volume, structure and quantity.

War is an illustration of this thesis, to-day it spreads across the world like a fire, and it is man who is in the service of war and of flight; the converse is not true, man obeys flight and war.

We are dealing, it must be stressed, with a visionary not a philosopher. But perhaps visionary is not quite the right term, poet would be a better word if it had not been so cheapened. Thought such as Picard's quite naturally comes as though from the secret councils of creation. It is no good asking him why he holds a particular conviction. The only thing that can be asked about Picard's books is: does a conviction of truth arise from his affirmations? Does this conviction help to throw some light on the disconcerting situation in which we find ourselves? I think it would be hard to deny that this is so even though the degree of light varies in his works.

Picard's metaphysics of Flight, which personally I should prefer to call perdition, is of exceptional interest in that it gives us a glimpse of the hidden and formidable meaning of a phenomenon of which sociology, whether Marxist or not, can give only a superficial interpretation. Indeed, Picard makes us suspect that this interpretation itself is only another manifestation of the Flight and another symptom of perdition. The act of understanding itself is at issue. To understand is to achieve a certain equilibrium.

Picard is amongst the few who can resist the universal vertigo and who appear capable of redirecting the remnants of the thinking élite. Without such a redirection it is impossible not to despair of mankind.

GABRIEL MARCEL.

INTRODUCTION

THERE is some danger that, faced with the false religion of Communism, we should forget that Western Europe and the United States are only exposed to infection by this false religion because they are already sick. How we are to diagnose this sickness is a matter of some difficulty. All the catch-phrases that resound daily from the Press and the pulpit have a certain truth in them. Whether or not we agree with this or that way of putting the situation into words, we see that lying within the shadow cast by the verbal formula there is a tiny pearl of truth. But precisely this is what slackens the will and overcomes us with a despairing sense of impotence. Whatever is capable of this kind of formulation, banal and abstract, is as dead as the moth in the collector's poison bottle; for our world is the world of the dead formula and if we are drifting

towards catastrophe it is with the formula of salvation
upon our lips. Abolish national sovereignty! Return
to God! Restore the joy that comes from creative
work! Acquire unitive knowledge of the Divine
Ground of existence! What are these but improving
and more sophisticated reflections of the archetypal
utterances that from walls and sky-signs and the
glossy pages of magazines exhort us to consume this
cereal to keep our bowels open, to use this cosmetic
to intensify our sexual charm, to take this course of
study that we may transform ourselves into highly-
paid business executives?

One of the great merits of Dr. Picard's *The Flight
from God* is that he has shot, stuffed, and mounted this
world of the dead formula, much as Mr. Hemingway
shot, stuffed, and mounted the professional revolu-
tionary of our time in his scarifying portrait of André
Marty in *For Whom the Bell Tolls*. The world of the
dead formula is Dr. Picard's "world of the Flight".
But is not "the world of the Flight" yet another dead
formula? It could indeed become such. If it is more
than a formula, this is because Dr. Picard is above
all a poet rather than a philosopher or a social
scientist. The function of the poet is different from
that of the philosopher or the social scientist. He is
always concerned with the concrete; he moistens the
throat dry with the swallowing of abstractions; for

what the poet says is as much a concrete and created thing as a painting or a tree. The work of the poet, like the charm of the world of nature and the majesty of the Liturgy, may be a means of quickening into life the perambulating corpses of the world of the Flight.

But what is this *Flight*, the reader may ask, what is this extraordinary phenomenon which, according to Dr. Picard, is present in every manifestation—art, morals, religion, politics—of contemporary life? Is it something real or is it just a way of speaking? The question is symptomatic of the habit of mind so exhaustively analysed in *The Flight from God*. In terms of the presuppositions that lie behind the question, perhaps no answer can be given; or perhaps one can only reply, as one might reply to the questions of a child who had awakened from a nightmare, that it isn't real, that it was only a dream. See, here is the reassuring light, the familiar pictures, the cool hand of the mother. It wasn't real, it was only a dream. Now, go to sleep again. Even the adult who says to the child that it was "only a dream" must at times reflect upon what these words can mean. A dream is surely something, and in all ages down to our own, the age of Freud and Jung, the dream has been thought to be as full of meaning, as pregnant with fortunate or disastrous consequences,

B

as anything within human experience. So we may
say to the enquirer: By all means think of the Flight,
if you wish to do so, as a way of speaking; but if
you do so it is because God and the Devil, good and
evil, dreams and visions, myths and fairy stories, are
"only" ways of speaking, too.

A hasty reading of *The Flight from God* might
convey the impression that Dr. Picard is a naive
person who thinks it would be very agreeable if the
work of the Renaissance could be undone and all
men lived in a condition of religious torpor under the
beneficent rule of Pope and Emperor. This would be
a radical misunderstanding indeed and would indicate a failure to understand the first sentence in
the book. The Flight is the predicament of mankind
in every age. Dr. Picard might have set beside the
epigraph from St. Augustine these words by Cardinal
Newman: ". . . *if* there be a God, *since* there is a God,
the human race is implicated in some terrible
aboriginal calamity." The Flight is the falling away
of mankind from God. But this is not an absolute
dereliction, for if there are those who flee there is
One Who pursues them. Paradoxically, the Flight is
even a sign of hope—*O felix culpa!* has been said of
Adam's fall—for the swifter the Flight, the swifter
the Pursuit, and He Who pursues will at last overtake
those who flee and, at the end of time, end the Flight.

This is said with such power and beauty in the last
chapter of the book that it may seem absurd to say
the same thing here and to insist, as though the book
itself were not perfectly clear, that at bottom the
Flight itself is a sign of hope; but my experience tells
me that whoever challenges the presupposition of the
age—that the Flight is a self-contained and self-
sufficient system with internal energies capable of
bringing about all manner of improvements for men—
is in danger of being dismissed as a miserable fellow.
If the Flight really were what the modern client of
progress and emancipation supposes it to be, we should
be the most wretched of men. But, over against the
world of Becoming, the world of process, of generation
and decay, is the world of Being. This world of Being
is not in the least like the caricature offered by so many
metaphysical systems. The fullness of being is more
concrete than the most concrete human experience,
more personal than the human person; for the fullness
of Being is, and proceeds from, the God Who revealed
Himself out of the Burning Bush. Then, He revealed
His Name to Moses as *Yaweh*: He Who Is—Self-
Existent Being.

Now, Being and Personality are communicated to
the created order from their divine source; and when
belief in this divine source grows weak and formal, or
when the existence of God is denied or ignored, then

the presence of being and personality in the created
order is denied or ignored. This denial, this ignorance,
does not constitute the Flight, for the Flight is
aboriginal, the universal human predicament; but it
constitutes that peculiar human situation within the
Flight from which nothing but the Flight can
be seen, a dark ignorance into which man is
plunged when he fails to see that, over against
the apparently destructive process of becoming,
there is that which does not change but which is at
the same time not static—this would be a privation,
a limitation—rather, it is the infinite ocean of Being,
the source and end of the energy of the process
of Becoming.

On the existential level, the level of common
feeling, judgment and practice, this immersion in
the process of becoming is characteristic of much
that predominates in Western civilization and
culture. There are, both in Western Europe and
the United States, abundant examples of other ways
of life and of other values; but the civilization and
culture represented by the juke-box, the commercial
Press and cinema, the mythology of modern industry
and commerce with its emphasis on the moral beauty
of lives devoted single-mindedly to the acquisition of
wealth, these would surely strike a hypothetical
visitor from Mars with greater force and vivacity

INTRODUCTION   xxi

than, say, the disinterested labours of scholars in the
best American universities or the simple, disciplined,
and religious way of life in a valley of Dr. Picard's
own Switzerland. Much of our way of life is trivial
and unworthy. This may always have been true of
human life; but to-day—and this is the modern
situation within the Flight, as distinct from the
situation of men in an age of Faith—the trivial and
unworthy are not seen for what they are. There is a
complete "transvaluation of values"; the hierarchy
of being is inverted; contemplation is for the sake of
action, not action for the sake of contemplation;
growing old we strive, aided by cosmetics and
surgery and catch-phrases ("a man is as old as he
feels"), after an undignified and unseasonable youth;
death, the great climax of earthly life and the gate
of eternity, is degraded to a level of unspeakable
triviality, and if we paint the features of the dead
and clothe the dead body that we may contrive the
illusion of life, this is because the reality of death, in
all its greatness and solemnity, is denied. Such is
the world of the Flight, the world of men "having
no hope, and without God in the world", in the
terrible words of the Apostle.

The virtue of Dr. Picard's account of what is
most characteristic of the contemporary world is that
it is not, as it were, a *clinical* account, a mere cold

anatomy of despair. Such accounts, such anatomizing, no doubt have their uses; but by themselves they do not set working the chemistry of the imagination. What Dr. Picard gives us is the vision of a man of powerful imagination, of poetic sensibility, of tender feeling, and of an invincible courage. Here and there men will make this vision their own and will thus help to rebuild civilization and rescue the world from despair.

When, in 1947, the present writer, together with his colleague, first approached Dr. Picard with a request for permission to attempt a translation of this work, the world was already beginning to enter the period of post-war disillusionment. The feeling of disillusionment has increased since then and, especially perhaps in the English-speaking countries, there is a common feeling that the framing of practical solutions to our problems is above all else important. This is certainly important and necessary work; but more than ever we should distinguish between the symptoms and the disease itself. *The Flight from God* will not tell us how to establish international control over atomic energy or how to create a *modus vivendi* between Russia and the West. What it exposes may be even more important: some of the roots of the distresses that afflict this tragic century.

                                        J. M. CAMERON.

The University, Leeds.

DESCRIPTION OF
THE FLIGHT

IN every age man has been in flight from God. What distinguishes the Flight to-day from every other flight is this: once Faith was the universal, and prior to the individual; there was an objective world of Faith, while the Flight was only accomplished subjectively, within the individual man. It came into being through the individual man's separating himself from the world of Faith by an act of decision. A man who wanted to flee had first to make his own flight. The opposite is true to-day. The objective and external world of Faith is no more; it is Faith which has to be remade moment by moment through the individual's act of decision, that is to say, through the individual's cutting himself off from the world of the Flight. For to-day it is no longer Faith which exists as an objective world, but rather the Flight; for every situation into which man comes is from the

1

beginning, without his making it so, plainly a situation of flight, since everything in this world exists only in the form of the Flight. It may well be that through an act of decision each situation of the Flight can be transformed into the corresponding situation of Faith. But this is hard; and even if one individual should tear himself away from the world of the Flight into the world of Faith, he succeeds only for himself, as an individual. The world of the Flight exists independently of his decision.

There seem to be no men outside the Flight. Man exists only in so far as he shares in the Flight. A man lives; and, living, he flees. To live and to flee are one. The individual exists in the first place as one who flees, and only after this and upon reflection does he discover that there might also be that which does not flee. The Flight is so much a part of himself that it seems to be the rule and not the exception. When the Flight exists by itself and independently of man, one no longer asks why one flees. One forgets that one flees from God.

In the world of Faith, all conflict, all wavering— to flee or not to flee—was *within* man: it is now carried over into the dynamic of the Flight *outside* him. The Flight has made itself independent. It is as though it had never dwelt within man. It has now come to be something with its own structure and its own laws.

So much is it its own master, that the Flight would go on even were man to forget to flee. No additional, no specific, act is necessary to make man flee from God. Once there is a situation of flight there is no more standing still, no more alternation between fleeing and not fleeing. The Flight is always there and is as much taken for granted as the air we breathe, so much taken for granted that there seems never to have been anything other than the Flight. Flight was in the beginning: in the beginning was the Flight. In the world of Faith, man is born that he may realize himself in Faith. Birth is the beginning of realization: but in the world of the Flight birth is the end of realization. All that is realization seems to lie behind, beyond birth. Now, with birth, something new begins: the Flight. Birth is the leap into the Flight.

Where there is danger that the system (*Gebilde*) of the Flight may suddenly encounter the spirit whence it has torn itself, a more rapid flight at once begins. Such is the daemonic character of the system: it knows at bottom that it can only move through the power drawn from within man, changing it into an external force, changing it so much, that one no longer recognizes its origin within man. At bottom it knows this, and the more it knows this the more desperately it flees—and the more desperately it

flees, the more sharply it feels its origin and the
greater becomes its dread of being driven back
within man and of being confronted with the spirit;
and the greater becomes its dread the more it en-
croaches upon everything and the more it expands.

To-day man need no longer justify his flight before
the law within him: for the "within" no longer
exists and outside there is nothing left but the
immense *mass* of the Flight. This system expands, not
because man flees more desperately: it expands
through its very size, for through its very size it draws
everything to itself. It is the system of the Flight, not
man, which decides the manner of the Flight. Whether
this system represents a flight or something else is a
matter of indifference. Only the mass counts. The
content has importance only in serving to increase
the mass. The qualitative is throughout transformed
into the quantitative—has escaped into the quantitative. The system functions only as bulk, mass,
quantity, and exists according to the law of quantity.

The thing which is increased beyond its proper
size can no longer represent its nature (*Wesen*)
through its form: it can represent itself only in terms
of quantity. The war, for instance, did not represent
itself according to its true nature (victory over the
enemy), but only according to its sheer bulk. Its size
was immense and through its very size it grew still

more. Men fell, alas, only that the war might aggrandize itself. They stood in its way, and so they were thrust aside into death, and the war marched over the place where they had been, marched on and on.

As things are captured by the Flight only in a quantitative sense, there is nothing it cannot capture. Like a living thing that feeds and assimilates, it assimilates everything and grows: everything is transformed into flight.

This system is so immense that what it draws to itself need not even be transformed before it can be assimilated. The dynamic is so great that everything, remaining as it is, is rolled along by it. One does not easily notice that one is being rolled along within the Flight. The slow peasants, for example, slow like the seasons and heavy as the soil which no plough can turn, are sucked into the Flight and do not notice it. They are no longer peasants, they are now something massive, broad, rock-like, rolling slowly and heavily in the Flight. Their peasant character is reduced to the external and quantitative, and is something carried along by the Flight, just in case the Flight should at some time be compelled to move slowly and ponderously.

Thus the Flight rules over man and uses him: man no longer rules over and uses the Flight. The Flight is sovereign. Man is no more than its servant (though he is the one who is most ready for the Flight, since he has fallen from the topmost heights and so moves with the greatest speed). He dwells within the Flight, delighted that by means of it he is being provided for. He cannot exist otherwise than by finding a place— any place—within it. He cannot even flee by himself, for by himself he lacks the strength which he can draw only from the vast system of the Flight.

It may be that once, and in dread, a man attempted to draw aside, that the Flight might not sweep him along with it. See, it comes, monstrously great. His head swims. He falls, he falls into the Flight, but his giddiness is swallowed up within the vast motion of the Flight, as if this giddiness served only to prepare him for the Flight, as if it had been no more than a waiting for the Flight. Perhaps, too, there may be someone who lags behind the Flight: he seems like one who wants to desert the Flight, but he has stopped only in order to consider at what point he could best join in the Flight; or he has been directed to this place to act as the rearguard of the Flight. Perhaps, too, a few old men may be there, moving slowly in the rear: they are like remnants of an earlier Flight and, as in a dream, they try to grope after the ryhthm of that earlier Flight.

Man flees, but above him there moves something

whose flight is even greater than his. In comparison, his personal flight seems trivial, and he no longer cares about it. This too is the work of the great system: that his personal flight should cease to be important to him.

There is more flight than can be fled. Men cannot use up in full measure the whole of the Flight, the everlasting Flight. Man lies down to sleep, but even through his dreaming and sleeping the Flight goes on; and when the morning comes it is as though the Flight had passed through a tunnel rather than through the night. It occupies the whole world. Sometimes it seems to have vanished but it has only sunk beneath the ground for the moment, for the ground itself is its property. Underground it creeps forward and suddenly it gushes forth in new fountains of the Flight. The whole world belongs to it. All space is, as it were, claimed in advance. The voice of the radio seems to be an advance-guard proclaiming all space to be the property of the Flight. From every quarter the voices return and report that lodging has been made ready for it. The entire space between God and man is filled with the Flight. No longer does the void of nothing lie between God and man; this has been transformed into the plenitude of nothing, the system of the Flight.

Everything has not yet been dragged into the

C

Flight. But precisely this is its greatest triumph: it is like a master who, because he is free to do so at any time, does not compel all things into his service. There is a self-confidence in the Flight, a conviction that all things must become subject to it as soon as it desires it. Like a mighty conqueror who leaves a few still unconquered so that he may at any time return to the conquest or so that he may keep himself in training by playing with them, so there are still a few things left outside the Flight; and they listen anxiously lest a whistle should order them into the Flight the next moment.

We have said that in the Flight all that is qualitative has been changed into the quantitative: that the Flight is now only a massive system, and that therefore it does not matter what is within, man or something else. What is terrible is that man is no longer even necessary to the Flight. It is no longer *his* Flight, for something else, anything else, can flee in his stead; or he himself can despatch something else to flee in his stead. He is eliminated from, cast out of, his own flight. Man, in flight from God, man who has every moment to renew his flight, for he is overtaken by God at every moment, man who has escaped from his own flight—where is he, where is man?

The cinema—there is the perfect Flight. That men may learn how best to flee, cinemas are everywhere

erected, examples of the Flight. The figures on the
screen are fashioned only for the Flight, they are
disembodied. Like one in a hurry who drops his
luggage, the figures have laid down their bodily
substance somewhere in the background, while they
themselves make off in the foreground of the screen,
outlines only of their bodies. Sometimes they are
still for a moment, looking backwards fearfully, as if
there was one who pursued them. Alas, it is only a
game, they do but pretend to be afraid. No one can
reach them, these things without being. And now, as
if they want to fool the one who pursues them, they
move more slowly, they even translate a movement
which ought to be fast into a slow one; they demonstrate slowness in the Flight, so sure are they that
nothing can reach them, these things without being.
Here in the cinema it is as if there were no more men,
as if the real men were somewhere in safety, had for
long been in safety, and as if these shadows had been
left behind simply to flee in place of the real men.
They only pretend to be in flight and even the men
who sit in front of the screen in order to gaze at the
shadows there seem nothing but dummies, arranged
to complete the illusion, while the real men have
long since departed.

THE CONSTRUCTION
OF THE FLIGHT

IN the world of Faith, man need not adjust himself
to the many things that could be, but only to the
one who is: to God. Of course, man also changes in
the world of Faith, but he is certain that, whatever the
changes through which he moves, God is there;
and because it looks as if man wishes to find out
whether God really is everywhere, his movements
are slight and timid. He is ashamed of scrutinizing
God's ubiquity. In the world of the Flight, however,
where man does not know what he may encounter in
the Flight, neither men nor things are uniquely
fitted for the place where they happen to be at any
given moment. They are fitted for everything. All
things have to be ready for every possibility. This is
why they are incomplete and are only prepared for
what some day they may represent. They are made
to occupy an intermediate position whence they may

most easily prepare themselves for every place through which the Flight passes. A thing's worth does not lie in its existence but in its capacity to be everywhere and to become anything, and the greater the capacity for *becoming*, the higher its value. A thing is not—as in the world of Faith—the end of a process, the reaching of a goal, the seizure of and the retention of an end. In the world of Flight a thing is nothing but a beginning, not a beginning of that which has its own specific nature, but a beginning of the manifold, the leap into the manifold. And only in this sense does it exist: not that it may exist for its own sake, not even that it may accomplish its own development, but rather that it may accomplish any development whatsoever. The outline of a thing does not tell us where that thing is; it simply marks the place where it announced its decision to abandon itself. A thing does not seem to be real, it seems a mere bundle of possibilities, an abbreviation, a concentration of possibilities thrust into the empty form of the thing and waiting only to burst out of it. Man himself is not there where he can be seen; this is only the place whence he starts his flight. Existence is only an occasion for preparing oneself to be everywhere. It seems miraculous that man still retains definite outlines and that the possibilities within him do not tear him asunder.

This is the world of the Flight: not the world of necessity but that of possibility. Nothing need be as it is; it *may* be so, but not of necessity. Everything is unstable and wherever one sees anything stable it is only a moment of coherence before the transition to the next possibility.

One thing produces another, not that the other may be given real existence but only that another possibility may be produced; its construction is intentionally faulty, so that a new thing lacking this fault must follow; but the new has yet another fault; thus there is always a reason why one thing should follow another. The flaw, the incompleteness, is no longer the impulse driving man to force a thing or a situation out of its incompleteness and faultiness into something final and exact; instead, the flaw serves as an occasion for producing one thing after another, for producing new variations, always incomplete, and for justifying the endless succession of possibilities. The flaw is the motive-power of the possibilities. Probably, though, the possibilities are spontaneously generated, needing no motive-power, for in the world of the Flight things can only exist in this condition. They may not enter in any other condition. Possibility exists above all as an atmosphere to which things adapt themselves. For one of the common deceptions of the world of the Flight is that no special act is needed to prepare for it: from the enormous volume of the Flight comes an atmosphere in which things and situations are being transformed without their being aware of it. One does not even try out which possibility is the best; the state of possibility is sufficient in itself. If one thing were certain, its certainty would be enough to shatter this world of possibilities. Therefore, the possibilities have occupied the whole world of the Flight in order to exclude certainty.

In this world there is nothing "impossible", only that which is "not yet possible", and this only because not all possibilities can be manifested at the same time. The man of the Flight wants to carry everything with him; he does not know what he may need on the way and he wants to keep it by him in such a condition as to enable him to throw it away with ease when he does not need it, and for this the state of possibility is appropriate. A thing does not weigh much in this condition; it is easy to carry around and easy to throw away in the Flight. It appears to man that nothing can happen to him, that he is fully equipped, and that, whatever may happen to him in the course of the Flight he has already experienced as a possibility; whatever situation he encounters he need not repeat the experience and, also, he lacks the time; he need only identify whatever he has

already noted down as a possibility. He becomes a
trifler, for he no longer keeps hold of the thing he
needs, but only examines it in a spirit of idle curiosity
to see whether it corresponds with his catalogue.
What then, does he still fear, the man of the Flight?
The whole of reality is dissolved into possibility and
even the possible is never there; it only appears and
disappears; and his only fear is lest the entries in his
catalogue should be incorrect. In place of true fear
there is in man only the anxious pedantry of one who
has compiled a catalogue.

In this world of the Flight man has nothing to do.
Everything is there without his assistance. All he
need do is to select from among the possibilities. The
man of Faith knows what he has to do *before* he does
it; the man of the Flight has first to construct it out
of the possibilities. The man of the Flight is the
eclectic *par excellence*. Man himself, if he wishes to
realize his own existence, must seek everywhere the
fragments of his own nature and unite them. Continually he establishes himself and continually, as soon
as he has established himself, he disintegrates himself.
The man of the Flight overrates himself, he has no
firm standard against which to measure himself, he
has only the possibilities. He can proclaim himself a
giant, since the possibility which is his standard can
be expanded to the very limit of his desire.

Since everything here is possible, nothing is un-expected, nothing is wholly different from the actually present, nothing is surprising, nothing has the enchantment of the unknown; and therefore the poetry of things, too, is absent.

In this world space no longer exists, for in every place, everything is possible; man is everywhere at once, for he may always stay and, at the same time, still be in flight. The identical possibilities are diffused throughout space, which is thus abolished. (There may be corners or cavities left over in space in which a fragmentary event may yet exist. The other fragment is elsewhere, and so one event is split and scattered into the various cavities of space and man hops from one cavity to another.) Also, the interval between God and man is filled with these possibilities; it is as though God, the utterly certain, were to be trapped into looking into the space filled with the possibilities, while man flees unnoticed.

We have said that one is at the same time in one place and yet in another. But the soul—is it here or is it there? It does not know. It flees, it does not know where it belongs, it is perplexed. If man does not think this perplexity of soul to be a mere possibility, if *this* should be a reality for him, he becomes a madman and the Flight ends here.

Time in the world of the Flight: there are no

intervals within it; all the intervals are filled with possibilities. There must be no intervals, for wherever one occurs there is also a halt and no one is allowed to halt in the Flight.

In the world of the Flight time is never completely filled; for while time is running out the possibilities spring up still more quickly. There always remains a surplus of unexhausted time in which there is nothing, not even a possibility: it is the void of time.

There is neither past nor future in the world of the Flight. All that was, and is, and is to come, is contained within it in every possibility. Here it is not as in the world of Faith, where present, past, and future are divided from each other and are plainly to be distinguished from eternity, where the present exists in order to face eternity, where the past is given life by the passage of eternity, and where the impatient future awaits eternity. In the world of the Flight, times are not ordered in sequence; they are jumbled up. Past, present and future are all of them to be found in every possibility.

Events or spiritual states of the past, the prehistoric or the pre-Christian, for example, spring up in the present from these possibilities and vanish again within them. The springing-up and the vanishing are one. On the other hand, much that will not happen before 1950 appears already in our own day*; but this is not prophetic nor does it represent a world beyond all time. It represents the jumbling of time in which there are no longer any future events, but where everything settles itself in advance, not as a present event but as the fragment of a possibility whose place might just as well have been taken by another fragment out of the jumble—taken, for example, from the past. So we live: the year is named 1934, but 1950 and 1850, too, are mingled with it. When do we live? We look for our own year. We look for it but we find only a new possibility in this world of the Flight, where everything appears before it exists and vanishes before it has existed, and where that which has existed is once again in the future before it can exist in the present; in this world of the Flight where everything springs up in order to vanish and vanishes in order to spring up; where to spring up, to exist, and to vanish are the same thing.

In this world one allows every possibility to approach. One does not control it; it disappears before one can take a decision about it. Where there is no decision, there is no earnestness. Man risks summoning up the most terrible possibilities; and no courage is needed for so doing, for where everything is possible there is no courage. He thinks they are

* 1934

without consequence, for they vanish so soon. All the adventures implicit in the possibilities engage man here. One attracts the terrible as though in fun or by way of experiment, in order to find out whether the terrible still exists, whether a terrible possibility may still become reality. War, crime, pestilence, seem no more than successful experiments, and the men who die in them, die as the casualties of an experiment.

In such a world, where reality is dissolved into possibilities, there is no guilt; whatever happens, it is only a combination of possibilities and so not an act, and the combination, as though in fun, wears a mask, the mask of war, for example. It is, however, not a war, only a possibility which arranges itself most easily behind the mask of war. Neither does one think of guilt; one only considers which mask the combination would have worn had it failed to pick up the mask of war, and behind which mask it may next appear. Yet in the depths of man there is dread, a dread so immense that it must crouch, a dread lest all these masks should only be instances of a world for which the most terrible possibility is being selected to become reality, and for which the man of the Flight is being destined as the ultimate frightfulness.

Where there is no guilt there is no repentance. If a man were to fall away from the world of Faith into that of the Flight and to make the act of sin real for himself, the ocean of possibilities would sweep away the act of sin and cause it to vanish. In despair he must re-enact the sin so that he may again have it before him; yet again and again it vanishes. Ever more violently he does evil and ever more abruptly it vanishes. Like one possessed he is intent on making it so monstrous that it may crouch before him, a monster incapable of movement. Alas, it is at least sin in its reality that a man desires to possess in this world, hoping that if at least the sin could be impelled into reality, all the rest would also return from possibility into reality.

There is no truth in this world of the Flight, where everything is full of possibilities and is therefore ambiguous. Neither is there a lie, for a lie would make a thing too exact, would arrest it too much, thus hindering the Flight. In the Flight there is neither lie nor truth nor any mixture of the two, nothing but possibility, out of which—according to one's need—something may be ordered, now that which resembles a lie, now that which resembles the truth. If (according to Hegel) Faith is that inner certainty which anticipates infinity, how can Faith exist where inner certainty dissolves into mere possibility and where infinity is only one of the many things anticipated by the possibilities?

There is no Faith in the world of the Flight. For where everything is possible, one need not believe. God is degraded to the status of a possibility; even this is not an impossibility. If, in the world of Faith, a man says: *There is no God*, the denial disappears in face of the affirmation: *God exists*. In this world of Faith where there is a real distinction between affirmation and denial, affirmation is the stronger. Because it is strong, it permits the denial to exist. One who cries: *There is no God*, must do so with great persistence and with desperation if he is to be noticed at all. He must continually tear the *no* away from the *is*, but again and again the *no* is brought back by the *is* and is swallowed up by it. And often, along with the *no*, man himself is swallowed up by the *is*.

In the world of Faith it so happens that one dies if one pronounces the *no*. In the world of the Flight one lives by the word *possible*. One risks nothing in using the word *possible*. God does not swallow one up, for here he is a mere possibility. In the world of Faith, were God a mere *possibility*, everything would be impossible. In the world of the Flight, however, everything is possible only because God is no more than a possibility. One no longer flees from God, only from a possibility, and man reserves for himself the right to give the name of the God from whom he flees, now to this and now to that possibility. One ventures very far out into unbelief, for this, too, is only a possibility, and one thinks one could—should it be necessary—quickly recoil into Faith, into the other possibility.

Dialectical theology has tried to take God out of this mechanism of possibility and to proclaim him as the *wholly other*, as one who is other than all possibilities. But it seems that this God has not the power of "being other" from within himself. He is other not through his own sovereign power, but only by contrast with the possibilities. It seems even that the "wholly other" so much the more keeps the possibilities in a state of tension by means of this contrast, and drives them onward ever more violently. The more God is shown to be the "wholly other", the more the possibilities toil after ever new possibilities. By means of their dynamism they try to catch up with the "wholly other"; they try to overtake the "utterly different".

There is no death in the world of the Flight. In the world of Faith death is a caesura, a standing still: a heart stands still and with its last beat it beats against the wall of the beyond, and from this wall there comes a recoil back into our world. For a moment the world itself stands still. Again and again it is still for a moment at the recoil of death. The world of the Flight has no use for this. Here death is different. It is only a vanishing unnoticed by anyone. Sometimes a shot sounds, a man falls. The shot is only a sign that someone has vanished. In this world death is no longer a certainty, only a possibility like all the others. And as one vanishes with ease, so also one comes back with ease from the dead. Whoever looks on another is shaken, for he sees in him a *revenant*. So it comes about that to oneself and to others one appears to be alive and dead at the same time and one does not know which of the two one is at the moment.

When one looks at this whole world of possibilities, how everything in it is without body, hazy, shadowy, one is amazed that so much lack of being can cohere as a world. One simply cannot believe that this is a world; one cannot believe that trees, meadows, rivers, clouds, can tolerate the sight of so much lack of being without being themselves dissolved into its haze. Already the rivers carve their beds deeper in the earth, the fields arrange themselves as though for departure; but they stay because the trees, extending their arms in defence like a barrier of spears, stay too, while the clouds have long since fled. It seems as though everything were unreal, no more than an image cast on the wall of the world by an enormous projector, and one waits for it to vanish.

But it is a world, a complete world, except that there is no longer anything real, there is nothing but the merely possible. The entire world of reality has changed into the world of possibility. The world which desires to sink into nothingness does not do so as God's creature, but as something petty, something unworthy of existence. This is the last tribute paid to the world of God by the world of the Flight: that before it sinks into nothingness it sheds its substance, that it sinks down as the world of the Flight and not as the world of God.

How can a believer exist in this world? At every moment his faith is captured by the possibilities and dissolved in them, at every moment he has to recapture it, and again and again it vanishes. Never was a believer so poor, for at each moment all his faith is being captured by a surprise attack directed by the possibilities—but never, too, was he so proud, for at each moment he regains it. But what can such a believer know of being poor and of being proud? He has no time for knowing, he is only taken up with winning back the faith of which he is time and again being despoiled. If anyone were to succeed in thus living as a believer, God would have mercy upon him. He would not suffer him continually to win back his faith through his own efforts. God would bestow faith upon him. God himself would do

D

this, were it only at the point of death, when the possibilities were making their final attack. Thus, all would have happened simply in order that God himself could bestow faith upon a single man. The entire world of the possibilities would have contributed to this end, and would depart as a servant departs after performing his task.

THE ORGANIZATION
OF THE FLIGHT

1

THE OCCUPATION OF SPACE

MANY men and things are to find room in the structure (*Gebilde*) of the Flight. Thus, they are not carried along within the Flight as concrete realities, for that which is concrete is solid, has bulk and breadth, is clearly visible in space. The concrete, therefore, cannot be exchanged for anything else, but in the Flight one must often exchange one thing for another. One cannot dispose as one wishes of that which is concrete. Whatever is to happen to it springs from its very concreteness. Also, such a thing gives out a force which attracts other things into its neighbourhood. It wishes to rule and to possess things over which it can rule; therefore, it requires space and more space than the Flight can allow. And this, too, troubles the Flight: in drawing other things to itself, that which is concrete does not permit them to remain as they are, it refashions them in conformity with its own nature. The concrete binds them to itself with an internal rather than an external bond; in the Flight, on the contrary, all connexion must be slack, and if, in the Flight, things and men are tightly held, then this is only permitted so that they may the better take flight, not so that they may remain united.

Man in his completeness has no place in the world of the Flight; only humanity, the abstraction, exists there. Man has an unmistakable confidence and an unmistakable activity; there, where he is, nothing else can exist, nothing else can happen; he securely occupies his own space. But humanity, the abstraction—it wanders throughout space, and at the same time is nowhere. It does not fill space with its growth, for it is only a claim that man should have the right to be everywhere; but one need not be there at all, for it is no more than a claim, a claim that uncertainty should have the right of ownership over everything.

By means of abstraction things are being eviscerated and this is necessary for the Flight. All that is solid must be cleared away, things must be made porous, transparent: one wants to glance rapidly from one thing to another and to flee from the cavity in one thing to the cavity in another.

This cavity, the work of abstraction, is an unreal

space, for nothing can remain within it, everything
is in motion through it, it is a kind of space in which
one thing is swallowed up in the void of another.
What a world this is, the world of the Flight, in which
a thing rushes through the nothingness of every void,
always in flight!

Through the continual process of abstraction more
and more emptiness is being created; an atmosphere
exists within which things of themself become insubstantial, and thus able to flee without the act of
abstraction being necessary on each occasion. Automatically things and men, as they enter the world of
the Flight, are being eviscerated. The man of the
Flight has no time in which to destroy one thing after
another. It may be that man, even the man of the
Flight, could not bear to empty every single created
thing of its fullness of being; it may be that if he were
to take one created thing after another into his hand
and were to destroy it, he would in the end, in spite
of everything, be reminded of the Creator.

So emptied of substance are things—how long it
must be since they enjoyed their fullness and integrity! One cannot believe that a real man ever
dwelt with these empty shells. As if cast aside, long
since cast aside, they resemble empty cans at the side
of the street; the real things must be elsewhere, far
ahead, and one presses forward to where the real

things are said to be; but one always finds only the empty cans and always one presses on more desperately—and this is just what the Flight wants.

Sometimes a man opens up within himself and within things a great depth, he blasts out within himself a profound abyss; it may be that he wants to conceal himself for a moment in the depths of the abyss, but it may also be that he has only made the abyss within himself so deep that the Flight may penetrate the lowest depth. For the Flight is exceedingly powerful and the depths, too, are subject to it and must aid it to flee.

Sometimes, however, it so happens that a man falls not into this void but into his melancholia; he is weary of the Flight and so he does not even fall into the void, his fall is deeper, a fall into melancholia. He is now as though in a dungeon, and the Flight goes on above him, and, as an animal in a dungeon scratches out for himself a hiding-place, so the man buries himself within the dungeon of melancholia.

2

THE ARTICULATION OF THE FLIGHT

The phenomenon of the Flight is so monstrous in size that it cannot be given an organic pattern, and even though there were a power that wanted to set the Flight in order, the power itself would be transformed into motion, for in its advance through the endless sequence of the Flight, from one stage to another, the pace would soon change into a gallop and thus become the Flight.

The word of man, too, would be unable to set in order the shapeless structure of the Flight. The word cannot gain entry into the structure of the Flight. The word is spirit and, though it can have effect where there is no spirit, if it so desires; just there, all the same, it can have no effect on such a phenomenon as the Flight whose very existence is to flee from the spirit. Not the informed word, but the noise without form, is effective within the structure of the Flight: the cry without meaning, the sound that is a bare signal, the whistle, the whistle of command. The whistle corresponds to this structure: shapeless, involuted, endlessly fleeing. God shall no longer reign over men, the mechanism of the whistle has replaced him.

There is not enough time to articulate anything, for there is no articulation without the expenditure of time. Whatever is articulated moves slowly; but in the Flight one must move swiftly: above all, everything in the Flight wishes to be in the forefront; nothing wishes to be subject to the delays imposed by any kind of order.

In whatever has an organic pattern, each part knows its own position and knows it at every moment. In the Flight, however, where everything is in a turmoil—for all wish to be in the forefront simultaneously—a man only knows where he is by a signal, a signal from without.

Man is so lost in the Flight that now he is merely aware that the structure of the Flight is there, but he has forgotten that he himself is there. There is something that flees, but he no longer knows that it is himself. *I, I,* he calls continually, calling to himself as though he were trying to discover whether or not he is still there. *I, where are you, I, my brother?*—and again he makes reply: *I, I.* Perhaps he suspects that there is one who searches for him and, as though he were anxious not to miss the call of the one who searches (in this situation of being lost he would allow even God to search for him and to call him, but only as a servant calls and then vanishes), he replies in advance, as though he wished to have something to fall back upon: *I, I.* He does not even know whether *he* or another at his side has answered, for in the Flight the distinction between one man and another is effaced. All together make one shapeless mass, and from within this mass man continually cries: *I, I,* as if it were possible for oneself to escape from the confused tangle, as if one could cajole oneself by means of the call into making the escape. This *I* does not purport to mean *I exist*, but only: I am *here*. Wilhelm von Humboldt says that in the language of some peoples the *I* is equivalent to *here*: all the people of the Flight call out: *I, I*, and mean by it: *Here, here*. They do not want to tell us *what* they are, not even *that* they are, only that they are *here*. Subjectivism, the crying out of the *I*, is no longer used to indicate the mode of an *existence*, only the mode without existence. Subjectivism has no more than a topographical value.

In the Flight a person does not distinguish himself because he wants to manifest his being; he merely wants to show that he is somewhere. Being is no longer supremely important; it is only a means to make the person externally distinct. The kind of subjectivism no longer exists by which a man, from the depths of his being, shows himself plainly before man and before God. Nothing remains but a kind of formal subjectivism according to which all being and all that is within being are used to give man a sharp outline that he may be aware of himself in the turmoil of the Flight.

Everything man meets in the Flight he seizes and uses as means of making himself distinct. Among the streets of a great city we find an open space, separate and distinct, to guide us amid the confusion, back to ourselves and to the others; in precisely the same way man makes himself separate and distinct, that he may be seen by himself and by the others.

A thought or an act is not valued according to its goodness or its novelty, only according to its usefulness in enabling the man of the Flight to make himself distinct; his purpose in making himself distinct is not that he may be given a higher value than another, but simply that he may know that he is in flight like any other. In this shapeless world of the Flight everything is exaggerated and falsified in order to be rendered distinct. The whole of existence is not left as it is but is exaggerated in the extreme, for only that which is extreme produces a clear outline.

The poor must appear poorer, not that this is what they want, but that for many poverty alone can give distinctness. The rich must appear richer for they have nothing but riches: a man sits there and stuffs himself with riches until he feels his own existence; he might just as well be stuffing himself with something else, if it were only possible thus to make himself plain and visible.

Many try to be more evil than they are by nature: they try to magnify the evil; they are in dread lest, not perceiving the evil, they should no longer perceive themselves. The evil is like a signboard which a man hangs out to inform himself and others that this is where he lives; he would not know without this sign, nor would the others, those who, fleeing, have, as it were, made a pact among themselves, that evil shall count only as a sign. Someone is here, someone is certainly here, distinct, set in this frame of evil. By virtue of evil one knows one encounters a man. It is evil that gives him reality, that gives reality to oneself.

Many become better than they have it in their own nature to be, they overdo kindness: they drive themselves into it, into an excess of kindness, simply for the purpose of gaining clarity of outline through this exaggeration and of perceiving their own existence. Kindness is not an end in itself, merely a means of tracing a form.

Truth and falsehood in the world of the Flight are not moral values, they merely have value as means of rendering things distinct: a man stands out against this background, a beam of light shines upon him whenever in the darkness of the Flight he suddenly speaks the truth, and in this beam of light he sees himself and is able to discern something, something that he takes to be his own self. Alas, he does not value his ability to discern himself in the light of truth. Falsehood for him serves the same end; it, too, is merely superficial form, not even genuine false-hood, and just because it is only used formally, he has no control over it. Hence, monster-like, it can grow and man can by this means give himself the appearance of immense size. And always it has the sharp outline of the truth: it is as though the final separation of the lie from truth, that first abrupt decision, had always been sharply outlined and still remains so, and always, as before that final decision was taken, the words seem to linger in the mouth, before a lie or the truth is despatched into the world, even into the world of the Flight.

One goes to the root of things in the world of the Flight, for such radicalism drives one to the farthest limit of things. What one desires to drive to the limit is nothing but oneself: to this, radicalism is only a means; the degree of radicalism is fixed not by the matter in hand, but by the need to make oneself visible amid the obscurity of the Flight. One is more radical than one desires to be, for one is not sufficiently visible to be recognized by another in the turmoil of the Flight. This radicalism is directed only to the form, not to the content. These radicals have nothing within them, they are mere outlines: one tremor, and they fall away from their own outline. But the danger is that whatever is new in the content is continually being reduced to mere outline. The content of the world is transformed into outline and so made void: here is the danger of this radicalism.

Man falls into corruption if he lives, not for the sake of his inner content, but only that through his content a corner of space may be clearly marked out. Man wastes his inner content when he is persuaded that it serves no other purpose.

The whole of man is now in outline, on the frontier; one catches sight of man only at the frontier. Philosophy has sanctioned this situation. In philosophical terms one speaks of the "frontier situation of contemporary man", one takes pride in the adventurous man who dares to live continually on the frontier. But one forgets that man risks nothing whatever, for he has nothing with him; there, on the frontier, what belongs to him is already transformed into mere outline.

One advances to the very end of being, towards eschatology, for the eschatological is the last frontier. Here, before the Judgment, everything must be made plain, there must be a final clarity so that judgment may be given. One even accepts the last Judgment, if in this way at least something can be made plain. This radicalism, concerned only with form, is an abuse of eschatology. Eschatology has gained popularity in the world of the Flight, the fleeing like to think in terms of it; from within it comes a loud summons to the Flight: one is drawing close to the end. Everything is already moving towards the end;

now men must keep together, together in the Flight; it is now useless to reflect any longer—there, at the approaching end, one will discover everything, and everything, one hopes, will there be disclosed and made plain.

3

THE FLIGHT ENDOWED WITH MOVEMENT

To be ready for the Flight, everything must be rendered mobile. Whatever is in a state of being is no use. Whatever is in this state is immovably *there* and wants to remain as it is: unique and resistant to change. But whatever is in a state of becoming is in a state of continual motion: it belongs to the Flight. In the Flight, therefore, all being is dissolved into becoming. From that state of being into which it has been placed by God and in which, on this account, it wishes to remain unmoved, a thing is brought back to its origin; but this origin is not God, complete and perfect origin and being, but its own origin in all its incompleteness: small, physically small, still uncertain of its own existence, still in suspense over whether it is to vanish or to grow. Man brings about the diminution of a thing, guiding it back to its tiny beginning, so that the smallest movement can make it disappear or appear once again.

At first it is tiny, then it increases until it is something full-grown and complete. While one deals with a thing in this fashion it is never *there*; it is thus always moving from one situation to another: its value simply consists in its having arisen out of the process of becoming. One has no desire to know the present state of a thing, one wants only to call up the image of all that it was before it became what it now is. One who causes things to leap up and down this ladder of becoming renders them flexible, ready for the Flight. So not even the becoming is itself a purpose; it is no more than a means by which things are rendered mobile for the Flight. In so acting man has no shame; on the contrary, as he changes a thing from one condition to another, he grows over-confident, thinking himself a magician.

Since one knows that a thing can be both large and small, the thing no longer stands securely before man; and on this account he lightly presumes to treat it in accordance with his needs, the needs of the Flight. And because all the stages of becoming are regarded with the same intentness, the trivial beginning no less than being in its completeness, one does not know which is the more valuable, the trivial thing at the beginning or the final greatness: the finished and the unfinished seem of equal value. The placing of the same value on being and becoming

makes a special valuation of being unnecessary and
no stage whatever of the process is treated according
to its own value. This is precisely what the Flight
wants: not to risk the delay involved in the process
of becoming, but rather to rob everything of its
value, to drive it back to that beginning where
everything is on a level, completely devoid of value.
In this situation, everything, just as it is, can be
carried along within the Flight and there is no need
to place things in any order of value.

Religion, as a unique phenomenon deriving its
validity from its mere existence, is intolerable to the
world of the Flight. Religion, in all its immovable
reality, is rendered mobile by being brought into
relation to metaphysics. The point of religion is
that it may be transformed into metaphysics, and
the point of metaphysics that it may give birth to the
science of the positivist: the only value of one thing is
that it gives rise to something else; what this "something else" may be does not matter, only the process
of change matters. In this way religion, as it glides
past, appears to be something provisional, transient,
and this satisfies the man of the Flight.

Within the Flight all history exists solely that man
may render himself and things mobile, and this he
does that he may cast himself into the past from the
present age, and, from the past, cast himself back

into pre-history. But, as one does so, one has no desire to linger in the past, only to cast oneself towards it. That which is past is of no account, only the casting of oneself towards it counts; and the use of history is that one can be everywhere and nowhere at once; and thus it is degraded into a kind of gymnastic. In the world of Faith, history is of use to man in helping him to rescue for the present whatever in the past has stood in God's sight, so that the man of the present may not stand solitary before God. In the world of the Flight, history is degraded into a mere ransacking of the past for things which can serve as the companions of man's flight.

This also is true. One presents the past as better than the present, or the future as better—or worse—than the present. But in the Flight this does not mean that one really places a value on them, for "better" and "worse" simply indicate the limits between which one shifts one's valuations. What has been constructed is a purely physical scale, not a scale of moral values. Things have to be rendered mobile for the Flight; and if they decline from "better" to "worse", they do so only for the sake of falling, and falling is understood solely in accordance with the laws of mechanics.

In this world, sociology has been made into a device for preparing phenomena for the Flight.

E

Sociology will not allow Spirit its own sphere of autonomy, it will not allow Spirit any independence of the situation within which it manifests itself. On the contrary it derives its validity from the situation. For example, Spirit is explained as the product of this or that social stratum and is thus deprived of its sovereignty. Here Spirit signifies that which changes as it moves from one social stratum to another. But it is not the changing *Spirit* which interests us, only the outer aspect, the *mechanics* of the change; it seems that in this way Spirit is being made flexible and mobile for the Flight. Spirit has been divided, fragmented: there is a spirit belonging to this and to that sociological group, each group having its own peculiar little spirit, exactly what one needs in the Flight, where, in order to flee more easily, one breaks the whole up into parts; and, as always happens when one separates the part from the whole and when one feels uneasy for having done so, one magnifies the tiny part, making it ridiculously important, so that no one may notice that the tiny part is not the whole. Here the social stratum is primary, Spirit merely secondary. The materialists, for instance, only allow Spirit to be a superstructure resting upon the social stratum, or no more than a kind of haze or lcoud beneath which the stratum moves in this or that direction. Thus, the ubiquity of Spirit, the

possibility of its being everywhere, is not within the
world of the Flight, where Spirit has to obey the will
of things which also want to be everywhere, brought
about in the same way as within the world of Faith.

The *I* existing in the world of Faith is an *I* that will
not allow itself to be absorbed by or mingled with
everything; it is unique, a single whole, unambiguous,
it gives an account of itself before God and before
itself. But this *I* man here finds inconvenient, too un-
yielding in relation to the mobile character of the
Flight. The man of the Flight, therefore, breaks up
the *I*, takes it to pieces, as one in flight takes a whole
to pieces in order to flee in greater comfort. And he
requires of the *I* that it should display this or that part
of itself in accordance with his needs in the Flight.
Not that these various components of the *I* have a
genuine existence. Rather, one simply attaches
different names to these different appearances of the
I; one designates them, as it were, and while one is
designating them one believes in their genuine
existence. First, the *subjective I* is detached: but this
same man also displays a *collective I*; and as if this
splitting of the *I* into two components, the subjective
and the collective, were not enough, a further part, a
primordial *I*, is detached, and he requires of this that
it should rescue for the present all that lies in the
distant past. And there is yet another part, a fourth

part of the *I* kept in readiness: that part which looks with a presentiment towards that which is to come.

But no component of the *I* is ever in itself firm and distinct; each tugs at the other. From behind, the primordial *I* tugs at the subjective *I* concerned with the present, while from in front the *I* of the presentiment pulls it onward; and the collective *I* crowds in from every side. Now this part of the *I*, now that, thrusts itself forward distinctly; the *I* continually varies, and endures by reason of perpetual change. On the whole, it is no more than a setting within which the parts are being exhibited. One supposes, too, that one can deal with the *I* as one pleases, for, disintegrated, in fragments, it no longer faces one as a single whole.

The existence of the *I* is no longer important; only its continual change matters. The man of the Flight wears each change like a mask. He takes pride in his ability so to mask himself with this *I*, whose primordial origin has been verified for him. Each new mask of the *I* is a matter for pride. The seriousness of the *I*, the fact that one's being springs solely from the uniqueness of the *I*—this seriousness is exchanged for a game. Alas, if it could only remain a game. But not even the game one plays with the various masks, the seeking after them, the playing at hide-and-seek among past selves and the singling out of them—not even this aesthetic game matters any more; nothing is left but purely mechanical change. The *I* is always *en route*, it cannot be found in one place. As a fugitive who wishes to evade capture stays now in this place, now in that, scattering clues everywhere to mislead those in pursuit, so the *I* hides, now behind this mask, now behind that.

Things and men are being deprived of their weight, and one might even say that in this way they are becoming so unattached that their return to God is easy. But it is things in the fullness of their being which belong to God, and only by reason of their gravity do they sink back upon Him.

In everything and in every man there always remains a residue which will not yield itself to the Flight. This residue devoid of movement constitutes a threat, for out of it can issue at any time the pause, the moment of reflection and of return; so great a threat is it that at times it seems as though this unmoving residue, and not the Flight, were the chief thing, and that the purpose of the Flight was simply to ensure that this unmoving residue should be snatched away and rescued from the collapse.

But new contrivances are continually being invented to give movement to the unmoving. For instance, one uses the passion of a man with depth of soul, a passion for the eternal, as a purely mechanical

force, that one may be dragged and carried along by
it. Many among the men of the Flight perceive the
enormous dynamic power of Pascal, Kierkegaard,
Dostoevsky; but they transform the inward dynamism
into one which is external, hanging on to Pascal, to
Kierkegaard, to Dostoevsky, as though these were
steam engines carrying them along. While the passion
of Dostoevsky, of Kierkegaard, of Pascal, moved
them towards God, for only through him were they
fired with passion, in the world of the Flight they let
themselves be for ever hurled from one position to
another. The former died of their passion, the latter
manoeuvre with it.

The system of psycho-analysis has been invented.
Within it all phenomena are understood in terms of
a single principle, the erotic principle, not because
they actually derive from this principle, as the
psycho-analysts allege, but because they do *not*
derive from it; and they therefore recoil from this
false principle and plunge into a vortex. Precisely
this vortex is what one longs for, in order by this
means to throw things into a tumult, that they may
not harmonize with the principle to which one has
attached them; and this inadequacy (i.e. the dis-
harmony between things and the erotic principle) is
used to drive things into the vortex.

One invents a device for feeling one's way into men

and things: here a man, in recognizing another man
or a thing, no longer takes the integrity of his own
personality as a starting-point. Rather, he breaks out
of his own personality and makes a breach in the
other person or thing; he feels his way, as one says,
through the breach, not in order that he may learn
from it, merely that he may have a reason for breaking
out of himself into another; all he wants to do is to
give himself mobility and (perhaps) to conceal himself within the other in the Flight.

What a multitude of contrivances for endowing
man with mobility for the Flight, to hide man and to
cause him to vanish! What is terrible is this: it seems
that whenever a man or a thing vanishes, God
vanishes too. God must be very great, to be present
continually, even though he vanishes continually.
Once a man paused in the Flight and his heart, too,
stopped when he came to understand that God can
show himself again as often as he vanishes and that
he can show himself everywhere.

It is love that holds man back from rendering himself mobile for the Flight. A man who loves another,
or a thing, contemplates what he loves with care and
for a long time, careful to discover in his contemplation if there is a part he has so far neglected to love;
and love is long-suffering, waiting until the beloved
grows into love. But all this, in the Flight where one

must be for ever *en route*, demands too much time.
And so the world is being systematically emptied of
love. All the relationships within which love can
exist—marriage, the family, friendship—are being
brought to destruction by the men of the Flight. One
tries to refashion marriage, the family, friendship, so
that these relationships may be merely external.
Here one is no longer held back, for here one no
longer loves; being together is simply for the purpose
of fleeing together. Only the abrupt movement of
love, its characteristic of breaking through to make a
sudden appearance, only this, the pure mechanics of
movement, is accepted: and one uses the movement
to acquire mobility, that everywhere one may move,
not towards the beloved but away from him.

There is one fear that is above all others: that
when a man meets love he may be reminded of God's
love in all its greatness, that he may gaze at God
and in his greatness find something not yet loved;
then the Flight would not be held back, it would
become quite impossible. And so one banishes love.

4

Man's Orientation in the Flight

Those in flight find it necessary to construct a
mechanism by which they may orientate themselves

in the confusion. In the Flight men and things are so indistinct and so lacking in substance that they can be grouped only with reference to their external characteristics. For instance, one divides them into groups with the help of the typological mechanism: one classifies men as pyknic, asthenic, and athletic (Kretschmer). For these typologies how man is comprehended does not matter; all that matters is the bare fact of his being comprehended. Typology is no more than a mechanism for placing a great number of men under one heading; it may well assert this or that about man, but the typology itself is primary, man is secondary, and in this way he is degraded. This, however, is of no importance to the men of the Flight, who ask of the typology only that it should stamp them with a sign denoting that they belong together and that in consequence they flee together. Thus, by means of the typology, the system of the Flight (*Fluchtgebilde*) can be seen at a glance; the system of the Flight is so enormous that one can never make up enough typologies: here the Orientals, there the Alpines, over there the Schizophrenic, and so on. Now the man of the Flight can let himself go, for he can always count on meeting a typical classification which will accept him and guide him onwards in the Flight. Such a man who is within the closed fence of a typology needs no looking after; he need not look after himself; he is absorbed by his type and despatched with it. Also, there is absolutely no time for the unique individual in the Flight.

Whatever cannot be brought within typology is thrust into societies, sects, associations. As in a battle (on account of the enemy's bullets) men do not stay together in crowds but fan out into small groups, so in the Flight men fan out into small groups and societies. The only secret binding them together is the Flight: all are comrades of the Flight. But ever and again some among those who flee suddenly vanish and are there no more; they are pronounced to be sacrificial victims: the Flight seems safer if a sacrifice is offered to it.

For the most part it is only necessary to let a slogan fall into the confusion of the Flight. Men then gather round the slogan and other men gather round other slogans and cling to them and allow themselves to be carried along by them. Just as many lights scattered here and there break up the night in its immense darkness into many lesser nights, so the slogans, like whirlpools of light, break up the immeasurable confusion of the Flight into small circles of confusion. The slogans are like meeting-places for those who flee: in the Flight, where everything is dispersed, a slogan is often the only thing which collects men; it is a meeting-place where they can remain together, while, at the same time, they flee onwards from slogan to slogan through the Flight. What is announced by such a slogan does not matter; all that matters is that it should be luminous, and visible at a distance. LIFE, in all its intoxicating radiance, here is an easily visible slogan; or MAGIC, bewitching and many-coloured magic; or EXOTIC, the "colourful" exotic. And for the most part the slogans not only shine out like sky-signs, so that they arrest attention in the confusion of the Flight, they also contain movement: LIFE, tempestuous life, contains movement within itself; MAGIC moves by the trick of transformation; and EXOTIC comes from afar. In THE PROBLEM OF THE GENERATIONS the young move away from the old; in THE DECLINE OF THE WEST everything slides up and down between the zenith and the nadir of culture; thus the mobile slogan fits itself to the mobile Flight. SPIRIT is being attacked because it is opposed to everything that flees, but so much tumult surrounds it that SPIRIT, even Spirit, seems to be in the midst of the Flight and to belong to it.

Above all, it suits the men of the Flight to employ symbols as slogans, for it is known that a symbol has the power of drawing things and men to itself. But they merely want to use its outer power of attraction: the symbol, employed as a centralizing

device, is abused in order to group the lost and
scattered men and things in accordance with their
external characteristics. It is not so in the world of
Faith; there, by means of the symbol, men and
things are taken out of the world of movement into
the world of that peace which surrounds the symbol
(this peace is the instant before the symbol brings
about a transformation). In the world of the Flight
the connexion with the symbol serves only to render
the Flight harmless; by means of the symbol one is
taken from insecurity to security within the Flight.

Otherwise, the most popular slogans are those
which indicate a polarity: baroque/classical; Ap-
polonian/Dionysian; soul/spirit; whole/part; old/
young, and so on. Such a slogan of opposites is not
only cast (like a fisherman's hook), as is an ordinary
slogan, into the confusion of the Flight so that things
and men may gather round it; such a slogan of opposites draws things and men firmly to itself. They
are held rigid within the slogan as within a vice. One
can flee undisturbed, one need not be for ever
watching to see whether or not one is in possession of
oneself and of the things belonging to oneself, one is
safe within the vice of the slogan of opposites; each
thing and each man is to be found in the vice, that is,
between the two poles of the slogan; the entire world
seems to be divided between them. It is of no im-

portance in the world of the Flight whether the things and men held in tension within the slogan of opposites are so held with justice or not; whether, that is to say, the things and men polarized between (for example) baroque and classical are in reality baroque and classical. The chief thing is that they are given habitation for the time being; indeed, the less they fit the vice, the greater the force exerted by the vice to hold them.

The dreadful thing is that the "infinitely great and wholly other", God, and man in all his littleness—are held rigid within such a vice of opposites—in the Dialectical Theology, that is. In this, God is no more than one side of the vice, of an utterly enormous vice, within which everything can be crushed—for it will hold everything. But God is not even prior to the vice; instead, one first creates a tremendous tension gripping everything within itself, and as one does not know to what this arc of tension can be attached, one places God at one end of it. The tension in which man is held is so great, not because God exists, and exists in the first place—where God is no vice need grip, for Love is there—but because tension exists in the first place, and one uses God in a secondary fashion in order to maintain the tension at one of its poles.

This polarized existence is pleasant to men. First,

the tension places them under no obligation, for it does not capture the true nature of man. Secondly, working like a stimulant, it squeezes all manner of things out of man; and one perceives how much one has within one, for now it emerges as a result of the tension. But one fails to notice that that which emerges is without value, and is without value because it was squeezed out by something—an unnatural and mechanical vice—which does not touch the true nature of man.

Such a slogan of opposites can only for a time hold man and things within its grip; it is soon outworn, losing the elasticity which enabled it to keep things together, for now it holds things and men together only in a mechanical fashion: it is like a worn-out spring. All the time the slogans of opposites are being changed round. It seems to us that in the world of the Flight the dialectical procedure is so popular because within it a changing round of the slogans of opposites follows automatically. Here we have the *first* position of the dialectical process; facing it is the *opposite*. Higher than both and waiting until the two opposing positions below have exhausted themselves, so that it may itself begin to function, is the *third*, higher position; and the very moment this begins to function, in face of it a new *fourth* opposing position arises, and at once above both these a *fifth* position arises, and waits for the lower positions to disappear, so that it can face its own opposite, until a yet higher position standing above both appears . . . . This mechanical process of dialectic, through which each thing continually forces itself into a higher and more glaring contrast, this process in which the slogans of opposites change round automatically, suits the man of the Flight. He can flee, and the landmarks he needs to take his bearings on the Flight function by themselves. Further, there is rhythm in the process of dialectic, and, like everything which has rhythm and thus has a certain order, it occupies less space. This, too, suits those who flee, this saving of space in the Flight.

Psycho-analysis, too, is in the world of the Flight a device for making the confusion of events visible at a glance: an experience, this time a sexual experience, is declared to be central (sex giving the experience that lurid character which it needs if it is to be recognized as central), and now, from this central experience, one looks down as from a watch-tower over the other experiences in their entirety. Of course, it is wrong that experiences should be grouped round the centre of sex, for they cannot endure it, they perish, they wither, they come to resemble skeletons. But this is just what the man of the Flight wants, to get hold of the withered experiences so that he may

carry a great many of them along with him, as though
they were cans of preserved food.

The figures of "Great Men" are used in a similar
way. In the fluctuations of the Flight, where
everything is infinite and chaotic, something large
and plainly visible is erected; great figures are to be
made visible! One uses them as landmarks, and the
great figure is only a point of orientation. One flees
again and again without knowing where one is;
then, suddenly, a vast shape looms up; the figure
of Napoleon stands there in all its biographical
grandeur; thus, at least, one stands in a place which
bears a name: Napoleon—and then one can flee
onward to the next figure. Never before have men
been given such grandeur as in the Flight. They are
gathered from the entire history of the world, and
biography has become an entire industry. But it
may be that the figures have been presented in such
vast size in order that the eyes of God may first light
upon these and not upon those who flee, first upon
the figures, while those who flee do so unremarked;
as though God's eyes could be directed to the places
where he may pronounce judgment and where
not.

In the world of the Flight, men increase the
magnitude of events beyond what the events are in
themselves. An event is not permitted to exist on

account of its inner content, but only on account of its being visible. It must stand out against the confusion and be visible from every point, for one wants to use it as a meeting place, to show that one is still there, and in this way a great event is like an immense rendezvous. In this world without form each event is exploited as a means of orientation. Events are genuinely signs in the world of the Flight; but they are signs of the Flight.

Here there is one thing more to be said. From time to time in the world of the Flight books appear and create a great sensation simply in order to be seen and read by all those who flee. For those who flee and disperse to every quarter, so that not a word passes from one to another any more, need from time to time something to re-establish a relation between them. *The Foundations of the Twentieth Century* or *The Decline of the West* provides such a relationship. One person encounters another at *The Decline of the West*; all those who flee meet there. Such books do not belong to literature but are useful in their outer appearances for the sake of orientation. When one who flees is ignorant of the other at his side, he can at least know that he can meet the other at *The Decline of the West*.

The dreadful thing is this. Whatever is genuine is only put forward as a means of orientation. When

F

that which is genuine stands out in the Flight, it does
so through its singularity and it is this singularity,
this standing out in the Flight, which is striking, not
the essential reality of the thing. But it makes for
happiness to know that all this is of no importance
to whatever is genuine. It exists as if in an ordered
world, not in the Flight. There it is and onward
it flees; yet even in flight it awaits the one who has
need of it; but then it is no longer needed as the
sensational or the outstanding, only as it is in itself
and in its universality. This, however, would mark
the end of the Flight.

DESOLATION IN
THE FLIGHT

IN the world of the Flight man does not exist as a single delimited being but only as a chaos of feelings, impulses, and acts. None knows where his own chaos finishes and where that of another begins. Everything merges into everything else. But when an event demands it, man constitutes himself by gathering out of the chaos whatever is needed for this event, thus setting limits to the chaos. It is not man in his integrity who constitutes himself, but a fragment of man only, and only for the duration of the event; then, he vanishes once more into chaos. As he is not bound securely to anyone, he can vanish whenever it suits him to do so; but since he who belongs to none, belongs to everything, he has to show himself whenever anything in the Flight so commands him. This is characteristic of the Flight: man, and everything which is included in the inventory of man, without doubt exists; for in the Flight one does not think of everything that may be needed *en route*. Everything is swept along in its train but nothing is consummated. Nothing is taken out and prepared for use except that which is necessary for a particular moment of the Flight, just as men *en route* never unpack anything but bare necessities. Man does not care to expose himself in his entirety to the perils of the Flight, he does not care for this at all, and so he has arranged matters in such a way that he constitutes himself only from one situation to another. Continually the man of the Flight constitutes himself, and continually he dissolves himself. The world of the Flight is not the world of creation and within it man is not a creature. God's creation is of no account in the Flight; man and the world have yet to be created, created from moment to moment and cast aside from moment to moment.

Here is an example. In the vicissitudes of the Flight, what is only an outward meeting between man and woman, a superficial situation within which two human beings find themselves, is proclaimed to be marriage; but this, too, exists only for a momentary situation demanded by some circumstance of the Flight. It is not so in the world of Faith, where marriage determines the situation. Here, it is the situation which determines marriage, marriage has no existence prior to the situation, and man and wife are conscious of their union only through the situation. By creating an uproar one tries to make it look as if marriage existed only for the sake of the situation, and people separate not because marriage demands it, but because in this situation nothing remains to be said. People do not look forward to being together in a new and transformed relationship of marriage; instead, they look forward to a new situation; and the interval is not one of calm, but is filled with preparation for the new situation. The whole of marriage dissolves into situations; these provide the landmarks of marriage; nothing else remains, and in the Flight this is enough. Marriage is measured by situations and not by years, and man and wife remember each other not as man and wife but as fellow-actors within situations. In the world of Faith there is no proclamation that marriage is only for the moment. Here there is one unique situation, that of eternity, and in face of it no other situation can be created. Here marriage is something enduring, something even prior to man; man is only the means by which marriage is made visible in time; and there is such eternity in marriage that within it the whole of human time does not attain to eternity: man and wife live upon the duration existing within marriage prior to their own existence.

Through the enduring character of marriage man is conscious of eternity; and this is its happiness.

In the world of the Flight love is not an enduring thing. Instead of marking the beginning of a union between two human beings, it is something brought out only when it is needed. For the most part, love comes in at the end, a kind of remnant appearing at the very end, when there is no further way out. Love is here one's last resort and is used to get rid of a situation with all speed, so that the situation may in the end be swallowed up in the mist of love. In the world of Faith love is not used as means of getting out of a situation between two human beings, for the situation already has its own order before love comes to it, and is capable of existing in its own right, without love. The situation has its own order and necessity, and love is something added to it, something going beyond what is necessary, an overflowing, added to the merely necessary and thus superfluous in the strict meaning of the word; and this brimming over of love is what makes for happiness.

In the world of the Flight the father-child relationship, too, has no permanence; the child cannot rely upon the certainty of the father nor the father on the uncertainty of the child. The father-child relationship is not the unique relationship between begetter and begotten; it is only one of the many chance situations which may arise between an older and a younger person. One has to make a proclamation about it for the situation to be noticed at all, and one makes this proclamation only when it is advantageous for those who flee to flee together, just for a moment, as father and son. Only then is the father proclaimed as such, and he exists as father only for the momentary situation of the Flight. But the child, the poor child who never possesses his father except for this moment, makes himself older than his years—in the Flight all children seem to be older than their real age—as if, not having his father with him, he strove to have with him someone older than himself. In the world of Faith the father is always there, even in the absence of the child, and even if he is childless he is always the father; he is something of a father to all men and things, and he is a proper father to his own child only because he schools himself to be something of a father in every situation. For wherever the child comes to, the father has been there before him; and so every situation has something of the father about it and so in every situation he can be a child; the father who is always a father helps the child to remain a child. (Childlikeness is not merely a closed world for children; it spreads through every situation, and is present too, with the father, who fails to notice it, thus showing his innocence, an innocence in which he encounters

the child.) But in the world of the Flight the child is
related to the Flight, not to the father. Here the
innocence is not to be found in the child, for here the
child cannot yet flee by himself and has to be dragged
along in the Flight. There still exists, in the secret
place where the child is, a clumsiness in fleeing, even
an inability to flee. This suits those who flee. The art
of not fleeing seems to them something of which they
are no longer capable and, because this moment
when one does not flee might some day be needed in
the Flight, the child is carried along that he may
teach the adult the art of not fleeing.

In the world of the Flight there is no friendship.
Friendship amounts only to the act of fleeing together
in which, when one helps another to flee, it is only
for the moment, and then one has to continue the
Flight by oneself. In the world of Faith friendship
lies in bringing out clearly in the relation between
two human beings that which is in itself not evident,
the solidarity (*Verbundenheit*) of all men. Friendship
between two human beings is a testimony to the
universal human solidarity and as such a testimony it
endures. Without universal solidarity friendship
would not be possible, but universal solidarity would
not be such a self-evident fact, penetrating into the
secret places and there burying itself, unless it could
rely upon there being this testimony of friendship

before which it can renew itself and from which it can once more spread in every direction.

In the world of the Flight dogma does not exist. Sometimes, but only when it is necessary to pause for a moment, a dogma is promulgated as a means of bringing men together. In the world of Faith dogma is established for all time and a lifetime is not long enough to hear to the end all that the dogma has to say, so one life must follow another until the dogma is comprehended.

In the world of the Flight there is no faith. At least, it exists only for the settlement of affairs; when it is not worth-while, when there is not enough time, to show an event in all its clearness, then one takes an event on trust. Here faith is a quick method of dealing with an event. But true faith exists not only prior to each event, it not only brings it into being, it also determines the degree of belief due to it. All events are arranged in a hierarchy ordered according to the degree of belief. Within this hierarchical order faith persists to the end.

In the world of the Flight there is not even the reality of death. In any situation it is no more than the final sweeping-up, which one remits to a servant, not wanting to do it oneself; one leaves it to death, the servant. But at times death revolts; he will not be treated as a last convenience, and he makes a sudden attack upon man in the form of railway accidents, explosions, earthquakes. The track of the Flight is torn up and man is compelled to pause for an instant and recollect that death is not the servant of the Flight, but its master.

Nature herself no longer exists as such; she is only summoned into existence as one happens to want her. Spring comes unwillingly, with hesitation, slowly. But all at once it gallops at full speed, all at once it compels everything to burst into flower and wither as quickly: it is not the true Spring, rather a season condemned to be Spring in this world of the Flight. This is the greatest desolation (*Verlorenheit*), that even Nature no longer bestows her genuine gifts on the world of the Flight; she no longer takes this risk. But, lying behind the world of the Flight, there exists in spite of all the true Spring; it circles round each particular flower as if it wanted to prepare itself to become the true Spring in its fullness at that moment when man shall have returned from the Flight. And thus the whole of the year is waiting and preparing itself.

How desolate is man! In this world nothing exists, for though love, friendship, dogma, are quickly fabricated, they exist not as wholes but as fragments, fragments of friendship, of fidelity, and so on, and these fragments are the only glimpses of the world one catches.

Not a single thing is *given* with certainty in the world of the Flight; and if there were something given it would not be kept in existence, for the Flight is without memory; everything needed is created from one necessity to another—no, not *created*, rather *manufactured*.

Man is proud of being a manufacturer, and proud that he must engage in a specific kind of manufacture for each situation. Love, kindness, fidelity, his manufactured products, seem to him novel, as though they had had no previous existence. And love, fidelity, kindness, all these, do not seem really to be there; rather, it is as though they were making a first or a final appearance, as in a theatre. A man on a long journey may suddenly open his suitcase and take out a few tiny pieces of wood with which to perform tricks for his fellow-travellers: in just this way, love and fidelity are taken out of the suitcases of the Flight, shown off in an extravagant and dramatic fashion, then made to vanish again; and one continues to wear an expression suggesting that there is a great deal left in the suitcase; and so one can continue the Flight in peace.

For the most part, however, love, fidelity, kindness, do not even exist as poorly manufactured articles, for they are only *discussed*. In reality, love, kindness, fidelity, do not show themselves, not even for the brief moment when the Flight has need of them; they show themselves only in discussion and idle chatter, and are swallowed up in them. Only this endures in the Flight: discussion. Discussion is prior to whatever is being discussed. It is the mechanism of the Flight. Within it everything can make a sudden appearance, everything is reduced by it to a dead level. When something is lost in the discussion one fails to notice it, for within it everything takes on the same appearance; everything, without waiting for a definite act, dissolves into the discussion.

But in the world of Faith, love, fidelity, kindness, have a real and enduring existence which is prior to the situation in which man has need of them. The man of Faith is happy in their presence, knowing he does not have to bring them into existence. For he knows, even he, the man of Faith, that he would not have the power to *create* the standards of love, fidelity, kindness, and at the same time to be loving, faithful and kind. Even for the man of Faith, this would be too much. Thus, even love, fidelity, kindness, are something *given* in the world of Faith, for God knows the limits of human strength. The man of Faith is grateful that these things are *given*, and that in each circumstance he receives more from them than he could contribute from his own resources.

Two friends, for example, need not in their friend-

ship begin at the beginning. They can live together
in friendship at once, as though their intimacy had
been a long one: for in the world of Faith they can
also share in the friendship existing over and above
their personal friendship. This need have no beginning, for it has been there always; and it is their
pride so to live together as friends that they do not
require the help of the eternal friendship, always
ready with its help, and in this way the eternal
friendship is kept new. A man could never show love
for another unless love were there as something
given, for only then can he be sure of the love which
springs out of his own personality, when it is a part
of the universally given love; only then does he know
that he need not prove that in his nature which is
loving, for the love that is given is grounded deeper
than he himself can be.

DREAD IN THE FLIGHT

HE—whoever he may be—who flees from God, knowing that it is from God that he flees, is in Dread. He can never understand why the sudden movement by which he broke away from God and hurled himself away from God has not torn him to pieces. He has no trust in himself, he cannot believe that he is still whole, a being still in one piece—and he is in Dread. This Dread is circumscribed and clear, for in face of the clarity of God even Dread becomes clear. Such a man bears Dread ever with him; he has fled from God, and now he clings to Dread. He has taken it in place of God; he cannot let it go, nor does he even wish to do so. When, for instance, he stands before a thing, he is not alone in looking at the thing, Dread looks together with him. Dread must share in everything, and he knows he must give a share to Dread, for he can no longer give a share to God. Dread is ever with him as a part of himself. As a man leaving one country for another takes with him a portion of earth as a souvenir, so is Dread with man—an eternal souvenir of his flight from God.

But a man who has *forgotten* that he fled from God, one in flight who no longer knows he is in flight, much less *from* whom he is in flight, such a one does not bear Dread with him; it is rather Dread which bears him with itself. He is now no more than an appendage of Dread, and everywhere Dread feels its way forward to discover where its creature may be; it searches for its object that it may establish the distinction between itself and the object and that it may discover the reason for its own existence.

This Dread orders man to mark out the whole space of the night with red, green, and blue lamps and to explore with searchlights those parts of the night which the lamps fail to reach. These lights and and lamps resemble watch-fires in the wilderness— the watch-fires of Dread! Around the fires men keep themselves awake with shouting and singing. Day and night are no longer divided between waking and sleeping; they make up one single round of waking. For day itself is no longer day that things may *exist* in it, rather, that they may be *scrutinized* in it; Dread commands day to be one bright round of scrutiny. Dread feels its way into dreams, and no longer

permits the soul to rest through the night, playing
with its dream-images. Instead, dreams are despatched
beforehand by Dread, dreams which sound the death
of sleep, and the dream is simply a spy in the service
of Dread. (Pyscho-analysis is the systematization of
this spying.)

But as Dread takes itself everywhere and grows
continually that it may make a thorough search in
every place, soon it ceases to know the reason for its
growth; it simply continues to grow greater and
greater until it seems that this continual growth is
the only reason for its existence. There is far more
Dread than one can absorb. Only Dread now exists—
man no longer exists; he has vanished within Dread.
God calls: Where is man? There is no answer, only
the silence of Dread. There is now an entire world
of Dread, and within it past and future are one
dreadful present. Here, everything happens just as
though in the real world, but it lies under the sign
of Dread, and everything happens by the order of
Dread, which knows everything better than man;
and man relies upon it. What is dangerous is that
man settles down in this world and no longer makes
enquiry after the object of dread, but deals with it as
something to be taken for granted. Dread is everywhere. Whenever man wants to make a beginning,
Dread has anticipated him, and whenever he wants

to bring something to completion, Dread snatches it from his hand and completes it. He runs to and fro in continual disquiet. Dread orders him to be in continual disquiet, that he may be prepared for everything. Disquiet is a condition brought about by Dread, for it has need of it.

(The Dialectical Theology is no more than a means for keeping man continually on the alert. According to this theology, *there* is God in his infinite greatness, *here* man in his infinite littleness; and the infinitely great and the infinitely little do not belong to the same order of being; they are simply borderlines, one in the heights, the other in the depths; and day and night the individual man is under control, whether he respects the borderline or whether he moves himself upward. In this theology everything is distrustful, in a hurry, breathless. If in reality there were this tension between Creator and creature, then the rest of creation would be in a state of tension, and every creature would be in a state of tension with every other creature, and one would always be attempting to measure itself against another. There would be neither peace nor persistence nor trust nor security; there would be nothing but continual explosions; men would always be under control and always wakeful, for in all the world there would be no more sleep.)

G

Man, no longer the master of Dread, is now its lackey. As a master stalks between two rows of lackeys, so Dread stalks between the rows of men. No, men are not even lackeys; they are now no more than walls, walls made out of what is physically external in men, their bodies, and between the walls Dread stalks. But Dread is also within man, and men are still held together only through the pressure exerted on their bodies by Dread, pressure from within and from without.

Since everywhere, within and without, there is only one thing, Dread, man soon ceases to know what is within and what without. Trees, the mountain, the tower upon which he stands—are they on the earth over against him or are they within him? He casts himself from the tower as if this were only a plunge into himself, confusing within and without in this Dread of his which puts everything on a level.

With the man of Faith, too, Dread is present, but not continually, for it makes an appearance only when he is in danger, when he turns from God without noticing what he is doing. Here Dread is like a messenger who brings man back to God and is no more than a means of bringing the danger to his notice.

Within Dread man wants to find out where he is; he wants to behold an object, an object of Dread;

DREAD IN THE FLIGHT

he wants to cling to it to save himself from complete dissolution in Dread. But no object can be found, only Dread can be found, and he finds it again and again. He distorts things in order to know that he has seen them, otherwise they would be dissolved in Dread. He lies in wait for his Dread to approach its limit. Beyond the limit he hears a murmuring; it is the sound of Dread, a monotonous, regular, uncontrollable murmuring. Then a new Dread begins, and this, too, he penetrates; but once more there is a new murmuring at the limit and a new Dread. The entire world seems parcelled out into fields of Dread, joined one to another by a river, the river of Dread. No ship sails upon this river; its surface is bare, except that at times a murmuring wave swells up. This is the sign by which Dread communicates with itself.

Man is able to do evil simply to fill the emptiness of Dread, so that there may at least be evil in it. Later, he builds a house of Dread upon the foundation of evil, that he may feel the solid ground beneath his feet. He experiments with evil; he tries to manufacture the most extreme evil, to manufacture the very ground of evil; and this he does because he will not acknowledge the true ground of evil. Sometimes it appears as though that evil which is being done is not only the evil belonging to and intended for the present, but as though the evil of the future were already drawn into the present for the sake of bringing into existence a great mass of evil. But Dread is greater than all evil, which vanishes and is dissolved within it.

Dread takes up the evil, without this bringing about any change in it. Dread is like some primeval beast able to live with or without eating; everything vanishes within it, nothing changes it, and it is then even more uncanny than it was before.

Once there was a great war, not nearly so great as Dread, and it, too, was drawn into the gulf of Dread. It had been made hard, angular, jagged, that it might stick in Dread's throat and tear it open, so that only war might remain, war instead of Dread; but war, too, vanished within Dread, and Dread remained. In this world the danger is that the greatest evil seems small measured against Dread, and that one can do all evil—compared with Dread it seems nothing. It suits man that in this monstrous Dread all sin is as though it did not exist.

Here sin seems to be the concern, not of man, but only of Dread. Dread and sin are to decide the matter between themselves. Man hands over sin to Dread and waits until it is taken up within Dread. But perhaps man has so magnified sin to bring about the intervention of God himself. The sin shall be made

so great that God must come in person to annihilate
evil and, along with it, Dread.

In this world *the* sickness is hysteria. Man cannot
stand a continual waiting for a surprise attack of the
terrible in the enormous space of Dread. And so he
himself makes the attack; he anticipates it, he inflicts
upon himself suffering of body and soul. He thinks
that now nothing more can happen to him through
what is terrible, for everything has already happened
to him. In this world no one is so happy as the
hysterical person, no sick person so little desires to be
robbed of his sickness as he does.

Man splits his personality. Never have cases of split
personality been so common as they are to-day. Is
not this indeed the most tremendous subject for
Dread: a man split into two personalities, two
persons facing each other? To whom do they belong?
Whose is the one and whose the other? Which of
them is being used? And is the right one being used?
Sufficient subject-matter for Dread is indeed being
created. Yet the answer to these questions is no
longer to be found in the world of Dread, but rather
in that of madness. There is only one way out of the
world of Dread—into that of madness. Many mad
persons seem like secret familiars of Dread: they hear
words and see shapes sent by Dread; they mutter to
themselves and only Dread understands them.

Dread seems to reveal itself only in the world of madness. It has extended itself to the frontiers of this world and has even crossed the frontiers.

Dread becomes greater and greater. This is the moment when, so man feels, Dread is about to seize the other creatures too, and the entire earth, to take them out of God's order and place them within the disorder of Dread. Already Dread is spying out cracks in the creation that it may break in and establish a secret occupation. Alas, Dread is cunning, too, and would like to seduce man so that, just as the Greeks sent the wooden horse into Troy, it may send a disguised Dread into creation; in this way, Dread can creep out at night and occupy the entire creation.

Man faces this decision. Shall he betray the creation to Dread or shall he seize Dread and strangle it? Already the pines that stand to his right and to his left along the way are pines no longer, only the dark fringes of Dread; already the river has carved itself deeper into the earth, the fields are empty, more empty space for Dread: man stands at the last moment of decision.

It may be, however, that the only reason why Dread constitutes such an enormous mass, a world, the only reason why it is gathered from every quarter and, as though it were a bundle of faggots, made into a single world, is that man may seize it, piled up in front of him like a bundle, and cast it away from himself and from the entire world. Perhaps this is the meaning of the world of Dread.

If man should succeed in seizing this Dread and casting it away, the act of freedom would be extremely exhausting. It appears that man must first create the world of freedom within himself, a world of freedom as opposed to the world of Dread, before freedom dare throw itself upon Dread. And if man at last were to create the world of freedom, even then the danger would not be over, for the greatness of this world might make him arrogant; he might seem to himself one who has triumphed and has taken Dread captive, who rids himself of Dread only when he wants to. Out of sheer triumph he fails to come to a decision to get rid of it; he keeps it by him like an animal in a cage, he makes a show of it and gives himself airs on account of it. He trifles with it and flirts with it, he becomes the showman of Dread. Such a man becomes the mendacious and trifling man *par excellence*. For him who once dared to trifle with Dread there is no longer anything to prevent his trifling with everything; and then, in an unguarded moment, Dread breaks through the cage and places him within its own cage, the cage of Dread, and deals with him in earnest. Man must humble

himself before the world of freedom; his having the
world of freedom to overcome the world of Dread
must make him not arrogant but humble. When he
is humble, Dread at once becomes quite tiny; he need
not even seize it and cast it away; it falls away from
him by itself.

Then, all at once, the lights of the city are no
longer the lights of Dread, but lights that await the
coming of God. Sirens stand ready to sound; everywhere there are those who watch for his coming.
The songs and clamour of the night no longer sound
that man may lie awake in Dread, but that man may
recall that God loves to appear unremarked and
suddenly, in the midst of clamour and unrest. One
no longer continues to watch because of Dread, but
because of God; and as, when a house is being
built, the workers hand on the bricks to each other
until the roof is reached, so men hand on the nights
across the days until they attain to God.

THE IMITATION OF GOD
IN THE FLIGHT

ONE tries to endow the phenomenon of the Flight
with the attributes of God, giving an imitation
of them within the phenomenon. That they may
always remember what he, the Pursuer, is like, that
they may learn to defend themselves against him, as
men who fear a surprise attack are always mindful of
the enemy's qualities and employ dummies in training
themselves for battle, just so those who flee want
always to keep before them the attributes of God,
the Pursuer. The entire Flight is tricked out like an
enormous dummy which is employed by those who
flee as a means of training themselves for the battle
against God, the great Pursuer.

The phenomenon of the Flight is endowed with
all the attributes of God. It is endlessly great: this
is its infinity, which appears, not as a mere attribute
of the Flight, but as its essence; the Flight is without

beginning and without end and since there is no break in it, man has no opportunity to ask whence it comes.

The Flight is endlessly great, greater than can be explained on rational grounds: it appears irrational, almost a piece of pseudo-irrationality, and the phenomenon of the Flight stands incomprehensible before man, a substitute for the incomprehensibility of God. The phenomenon of the Flight appears great beyond all human measure, so that there is no human word with which to name it: here is an imitation of the impossibility of naming God. The Flight appears so immeasurable that one cannot imagine it as having any first cause; it is like a self-created system in which cause and existence are one.

As in the world of Faith things exist through the existence of God, so in the world of unbelief things exist through the system of the Flight and are in flight through the system of the Flight. The system flees beyond all individual fleeing things and is thus a justification of the fleeing thing and the fleeing man.

The man in flight is surrounded by this system at every point, and the system is more powerful than the individual man himself, and everywhere there is that which flees more swiftly than the individual man, something which can only be felt, not grasped, and even through this it has power. The monotonous character of the Flight, as it feels its way, produces a kind of humming noise which continually gives notice of itself and vanishes without having existed and which, as the Flight hurries past, appears to be in control of the man of the Flight, keeping him in a state of continual disquiet. This humming of the Flight as it feels its way is an imitation of conscience, a warning never to forget the Flight—as though it were necessary to utter a warning when the warning and the Flight are one and when conscience is only imitated in order to demonstrate the power of the Flight to imitate everything. As in the world of Faith God is the unique certainty, so is the phenomenon of the Flight the unique certainty. Here nothing is certain but the Flight which was, and is, and shall be. It is unchangeable, everything is received into it and transformed; only the Flight itself remains, the unchangeable and everlasting Flight.

It is God who is being imitated, God, the background of the whole of existence. Just as (in the world of Faith) God is the background from which man moves into the world and against which man stands out (for only against the background of God does man's appearance become distinct), so here the phenomenon of the Flight is man's background; but man does not stand out distinctly before it; instead he flickers, lacking definite outlines, and he hurls himself onward, fleeing ever more swiftly so that at least the swifter Flight may stand out against the slower Flight which lies behind him.

The phenomenon of the Flight is everywhere: this is an imitation of God's ubiquity. But while in the world of Faith man can only be *here* or *there* and while every movement from one situation to another is an event (for in another situation one again confronts God's ubiquity), the man within the Flight is now here and now there, and at the same time he is neither here nor there but is everywhere: he is the man who is here and yet he is at the same time a spectre who is everywhere—the man of the Flight giving an imitation of God's ubiquity.

But while the world's space expands through God's presence (this cannot be otherwise, for the frontiers recede and space expands when God enters it), through the Flight it diminishes, for it is being exhausted as the air is being exhausted by man's breathing. Things shrink within it, and as they shrink an empty space forms above them: the heaven of emptiness which overarches the Flight.

The world of the Flight exists as a whole world—and someone must be above this world too, someone who has created it, just as there is one who has created the world of Faith. It is so immense that there must be a supernatural being there: he, the god of the Flight. Thus one gives an imitation of God the Creator. Someone must also have predestined it to flee. Someone, too, there must be who has placed man within the Flight just as God has placed man upon earth. He, too, must be the one who holds the entire Flight together. For how could this disintegrating, dissolving, insubstantial thing hold together if it were not held together by a god of the Flight?

Here one is not only commanded to flee, one is also told how one is to flee; this is an imitation of God's authority. Man is obedient to the god of the Flight and yet, having constructed the vast system of the Flight, he is at the same time its master. At one and the same time he is the creator and the creature of the Flight, and he is delighted to be passed backwards and forwards between that mode of existence in which he is the master and that in which he is the servant. This he finds delightful, as though it were a kind of aesthetic pastime. The man of the Flight tolerates even the imitation of authority only in the feebler form presented by the aesthetic pastime.

This god of the Flight gives an imitation of God's patience, but while God has love within himself that his unyieldingness may be relaxed, this god yields without love, he flees and is dissolved: his yielding is purely mechanical.

There is an imitation of the unpredictable ways of God. In the course of the Flight, in the midst of peace, suddenly a war appears. No one has expected it; and it vanishes just as suddenly. The Flight must be a monstrous thing, for a war to appear in the midst of it. One has already explored every crevice and has failed to discover a war! Unexpected inventions suddenly appear in the midst of the Flight: infant prodigies make their sudden appearances; new diseases, new epidemics, show themselves; sects appear suddenly and vanish once again; fresh ideas spring up; new movements in art issue from the Flight and stream past, one after the other. But whatever appears has no value on account of its being *there*, but only on account of the abruptness of its appearance. Only this abruptness is of interest, the quick movement with which a thing shows itself, the purely mechanical movement. This purely mechanical abruptness is an imitation of the unpredictable ways of God. But God is thus unpredictable simply because the instant in which he appears and sends something into the world belongs not to time but to eternity. In the world of those who flee, there is no time and, therefore, no eternity. In

place of the instant of eternity, there is a purely
mechanical abruptness and in place of eternity there
is boredom.

Just as in the world of Faith time exists over
against eternity and may at any moment be interrupted by it, so in the world of the Flight boredom
exists over against abruptness and is interrupted by
it. The boredom of the Flight flows onward in a broad
stream, interrupted every second by a fresh abruptness: boredom is continually being transformed into
abruptness, so that abruptness itself becomes boring
and commonplace.

There is an imitation of God's omniscience. In the
world of the Flight one knows more about a thing
than the thing itself contains; for just as everything
is connected with everything else, so everything dissolves into everything else, and thus there is always
more within a thing than really belongs to it. But
this "more" is the superfluity of that Nothing within
which all things in the Flight have been dissolved.
This omniscience is able to know all about things
because they have all become equal in nothingness.
When a thing is in flight, one cannot really learn
anything about it. All the same, a truth does at
times become visible, for in the dissolution of the
Flight things which belong to each other can be
blown together through some chance combination;

and truth is dragged down to the level of this chance combination.

There is an imitation of God's synoptic vision. Like a god, man directs his gaze over things far into the distance. He glances now at this, now at that, not because he prefers this or that, but because he wants to show that, like a sovereign god, he has the power to choose what he wants; and, in order to show his power, he brings together those things which are farthest from one another and which do not match one another. For the imitator of God and of his synoptic vision, time and space do not count: the Mycenaean period, the Thinite period, the Shang Dynasty of China, are linked up with the Frankish Empire of Charlemagne, with the Visigothic Empire of Eurich, and with the Russia of Peter (Spengler). Synoptic visions of the world are continually being announced. It almost seems that the true God can learn from this how to direct his gaze over the world, that he cannot bear to look at the world in any other fashion than that which is here authorized. In this world things are of secondary importance; their existence, their being, is of no account; all that counts is the relation within which they have been established by the synoptic vision: they are simply material to be related. Things are placed under orders: the whole of *The Decline of the West* is an order to world history to occupy the situation of decline, so that man, imitating God, may enjoy a synoptic vision of world history. One demands heroism of things, not that the heroic may really exist, but that by means of heroism things and men may come to acquire a similar bearing. Then the gaze of the imitator of God can easily bring whatever is similar into relation. But things are not always ordered to imitate *one* thing. Alternately they must imitate now this, now that, to-day the heroic, tomorrow the social, then the eschatological, according to the pleasure of their overseeing master; and this arbitrary ordering, now of one thing, now of another, is an imitation of God's sovereignty. Under these orders many things and many men perish; they are the appropriate victims and the entire Flight is filled with them. How great and how divinely powerful must this Flight be, to take as victims all these things and all these men!

It was unnecessary for man to exert himself so greatly in order to unite things; his voice need not have issued its commands so peremptorily, as though there were some difficulty in bringing things together. For already things are proceeding (in the world of the Flight they are always *en route*) towards one another; they dissolve and one merges into another; and so the entire display of giving orders is comic;

H

man, whenever he imitates God, is not only blasphemous, but also comic.

There is an imitation of God as Creator. Everything is returned to its beginning, its origin; but this is not done as in the world of Faith, that God may try them in order to find out whether they remain as he created them, but simply that they may exist in a condition of beginning. (It is agreeable to man that they should be at the beginning, for there they escape trial, since one can only try that which is completed.) What the Flight wants is this: to be primal, original, creative, as God is. The category of revolution is used to bring about the original and creative situation. The point of revolutionizing things is not that they may be rendered different, but that they may be returned once again to the beginning. Whatever is primitive is emphasized in culture, in art, in history. Man wants to be present at every beginning, imitating the Creator who is present at every beginning. The Chthonic, that which springs out of the earth, and, in general, whatever is dark, these are popular. Darkness exists before the light of the created; it is the moment prior to creation. Best of all, one would like to enclose the entire Flight in the darkness existing before creation, so that over all there may brood the atmosphere of the beginning, for then, at the beginning, there can be no one but the God who creates everything. And so it is, for a world devoid of everything feels itself akin to the beginning where as yet nothing exists. In the world of Faith man could not tolerate being so near the true beginning. He not only needs the beginning, even more he needs history, that which follows the beginning, so that there may be a visible gap between himself and the divine beginning.

Here, where everything is brought back to the beginning, sex and procreation are also emphasized. They are used to produce the atmosphere of the beginning, and so count for much. This is where the significance of psycho-analysis in the Flight comes from. It is a school to prepare one for the mock beginning, the pseudo-procreative, the pseudo-divine. One learns to bring things back to where they were created, that thence one may, like a god, direct them into the world. Procreation is not important because a thing may come into existence, but because in it that which is creative may be imitated. In psycho-analysis the degree of imitation is such that it appears as something excessive, not human. In this way it contrives to appear as metaphysics, for it seems that only in the sphere of metaphysics can the sexual achieve such weight. A god who permits this must exist; and this is the god of the Flight.

Man rends himself, exposing his inner being, so

that the abyss of nothingness may be produced; and this, too, is an imitation of the abyss of nothingness prior to creation. However, man is not, in fact, on the verge of the abyss, for it is an artificial product, and the darkness within him, the darkness prior to creation, is an artificial product. High above, in the Flight, he hovers, and below him lies the abyss. He blasts the abyss to ever greater depths, that the Flight may rise to ever greater heights above it. Man wants to hover, like the Spirit of God, above his own abyss. To ever greater depths he blasts the abyss. It is as though he tries to blast so deeply that the Flight gazing down into its own abyss may be seized with vertigo and plunge into it, and so vanish.

In the Flight there is an imitation of the entire being of God. But it may be that God, in his loving-kindness, has left this as a way out for those who flee, that they may once again find their way back from the imitation to the essential truth.

ECONOMICS IN THE WORLD
OF THE FLIGHT

IT is said that the economic crisis arises out of man's inability to see the whole structure of the economic system, a structure which is far too large; that the economic crisis is a crisis of humanity, that man has lost his own standard and that he can therefore no longer determine the character of the economy in accordance with human standards. It looks to us, however, as though man does not mind this loss of a standard. The human crisis lies not only in the loss of a standard, but, above all, in that this loss suits man and that he makes use of it. It suits him that the structure of the economic system should be so immense that he can no longer see it as a whole. In front of him there is something greater than he, something uncanny. It seems that there cannot possibly be enough human beings to fill the factories, to use the products, to put money into circulation.

91

One cannot explain economic expansion by an
economic motive. No economic aim is so necessary
to man that it justifies this expansion. The economic
system expands independently, of necessity; the
expansion is an independent phenomenon; the
economic system desires before everything to expand
and take possession of everything. Real things, as,
for example, a factory, are mere droplets in this
enormous expansion.

What is such a factory in the great expanse of the
economic system! It is now only of secondary importance that something is produced in the factory.
What is of primary importance is that in the factory
one gets a feeling of the infinite expanse of the
economic system. Such a factory is for the man of
the Flight as much an opportunity to sense this
infinity as is, for the believer, a church in which he
senses the infinity of God. Once they have entered
the factory, all men seem transformed; a single individual feels more important, just as if each one
had to carry out an order which had been secretly
entrusted to him. They are officials who do not
associate with ordinary people, who only now and
then make a slight verbal contact with them. They
pass like the priests of a god; they appear suddenly
from behind the locked doors of rooms and vanish
once again behind them, And, above all, in a

special room, never seen by anyone, he whom no one has ever seen sits enthroned, the Highest of all, called creator in the sanctuary of the factory and director in the ordinary outside world. One is farther off from this Highness than from God's Highness; one gladly subordinates oneself to him.

Although rooms in the factory appear to be infinite, although the only reason for one factory's coming to an end is that another may be started, and although the interval between the factories is one of sheer vacancy and not an interval of distinct space, yet all this infinity is nothing but an artificial infinity, which man has fabricated for himself and with which he toys, seeming infinite to him only because it is unrelated to any reality and because it is immeasurable. The economic system seems irrational only because man, in constructing it, sets it against his own standard of measurement. It is an artificial, a fabricated irrationality, made like any other machine-product. The irrationality is not primary but only secondary, reason having previously destroyed itself so that the incomprehensible may be made artificially. While the individual man helps in his work to make up this system, greater than he can comprehend, he is participating in a pseudo-metaphysical world from which he is not separated. He is not, as he is in the true metaphysical world of God,

dependent on Grace; instead, he collaborates with
and makes the system just as he makes some chemical
product; but he makes it according to such dimensions
and under such conditions that he no longer has a
complete understanding of why he makes it, and so
it becomes incomprehensible and irrational.

This appearance of incomprehensibility functions,
not only so long as man takes part in the process of
work, but also afterwards, when he is outside the
factory, and then even more effectively. For just as
the process of work is distinct from man's nature,
occupying only a part of him (that part which is
active in the factory), while outside the factory this
part is as though it did not exist, as though it had
been left behind in the factory, so from outside
everything that goes on in the factory seems to man
to be remote, desiring the indefinable and sharing in
it, and, as a part of him, continues to work inside
while he is on the outside. That part of man which
helps in the task of bringing the incomprehensible
into existence has nothing to do with everyday life
outside the factory. It is the other and better part.
When he enters the factory, man feels he is no longer
the same, that by means of that part of him which
remains in the factory he is transformed as soon as
he enters. Here he finds that which is *other*, which has
nothing to do with the everyday world. It is *his*

"other", waiting for him and belonging only to him. What need has he of the divine "other"?

Men busy themselves about economic affairs with great fury, as if nothing else existed and as if there were no Flight, and they hope that he who pursues them will not dare to chase them away from economic affairs in which they have buried themselves so deeply, and they hope the Pursuer will not notice that these busy fellows are in flight, that he will rush past them and fail to notice their presence. They concern themselves so furiously with economic affairs that it looks as though everything with which they were once concerned was only a way of getting into practice for economic life. Grief, care, dread, despair on account of God, seem only a kind of getting into practice for grief, care, dread, despair, on account of economic life.

Like an autonomous structure which determines its own size, the economic system takes hold of everything. Everything must enter into some relation with it, even things which are not really within its scope are drawn towards it. Because things outside the scope of economics are nevertheless brought into an economic relationship, the power of the system appears to be absolute, and its power appears to be the more absolute the less things really belong to it. The economic system is the lord to whom everything belongs, and as it reigns over things which do not really belong to it, the economy appears to be something which holds things together by an inexplicable, an uncanny force, not by a force which can be explained. It thus takes on the appearance of something transcendent, and, more and more, man bows down before the system.

What else can he do but bow down before it? He does not understand the words by which it names itself. There is only a great and mighty system to which one applies a few terms: stocks and shares, stabilization, foreign exchange . . . . The individual man does not understand the terms and the thing itself seems to him a nameless and therefore uncanny system. But he uses these terms (stabilization, foreign exchange, and so on) just as if he understands them. The merchant, the manufacturer, the banker, all see that the words mean something quite different from the reality of the thing. Hence it seems to them monstrous in the highest degree that the thing itself should exist and function, while the word, the concept, which is to denote the thing does not refer to it at all. To them it seems monstrous that a thing should function out of its own resources without there being a human word to denote it. And the economic system moves onward, like some nameless primeval phenomenon, some god-like being. Man now has for the economic system a reverence which he no longer has for God (he, too, transcends his name). For the economic system itself resembles a monster, and in front of it there is something tiny which, like a little dog barking at the moon, barks out its ideas. For the economic system, this discrepancy between its essence and the concepts by which one tries without success to define it is a stimulus to increase its autonomy and to become still more powerful. But for man, this discrepancy is a state of tension which he transfers from the economic system to himself and to everything else and by means of which he can, like bending a bow, increase his own tension and that of things. Man can have no greater desire than to shatter this general state of tension existing wherever things are in any way brought together. Everything must become relaxed for the man of the Flight.

The economic system has become so monstrously big that its functioning no longer depends upon its content but only upon its sheer mass; that is, upon a purely quantitative phenomenon. The contents of the system, the data of economics, are no longer able to characterize the economic system and to give it form. It exists independently of its content. Whatever substance may be brought within the category of the quantitative is a matter of indifference to the

economic system. That which happens to the
economic system, its loss of being and its transformation into something merely quantitative, might
happen to anything and does in fact happen whenever it is necessary. But it suits man to transform
economics into a purely quantitative system, for of
all things it is the most easily prepared for the
transition to the quantitative and has therefore the
strongest impulse to expand, seizing everything and
assimilating most things with the greatest ease.

This breaking down of being into mere quantity
suits the man of the Flight. Even when he stations
himself simply in order not to remain with God; that
is, when he stations himself in the economic system,
even there he is still afraid of being detained. Thus
the lack of being in the economic system, a lack in
which it resembles the Flight itself, suits him, for if
the system still retained a genuine content, and thus
a real nature, it would have the power to detain him.

Wherever, as in the economic system, great masses
of men and things are brought together, it always
happens that parts of them collide one with another
and thus are shattered; then a crisis follows. Or parts
may meet which fit together and strengthen one
another; then a boom follows. This see-saw motion,
this tension between the highest point and the lowest,
sets the masses within the economic system in motion.

As we said, there is nothing the man of the Flight likes better than this transformation of things into mere quantities. Here this means that the economic system no longer counts as such; it is a purely quantitative mass, and the mass itself now counts only as a movement—that is, the see-saw motion of the crisis. The automatic character of the movement suits man, for it means that it is in no need of his help; and so he can flee by himself while the economic system goes on functioning alone.

Precisely this automatic see-saw motion of the economic system functioning independently of man gives to the system the appearance of being independent, lofty, a true being, set above man. Suddenly, and contrary to all calculation, a crisis appears, and it seems that the magnitude of the crisis is far greater than can be accounted for by the economic system alone and that the onslaught of the crisis is far more violent than it could be if the onslaught were launched simply from the economic system. When the slump is over and when what one calls the boom arrives, the boom is usually as unexpected as was the crisis, arriving contrary to all calculations, descending like a blessing from beyond the economic sphere; and just as the violence of the crisis was greater than could be anticipated and explained in terms of economics, so the boom, too,

is more violent than can be explained on the basis of
the economic situation itself. Boom and slump acquire
an appearance of unreality, of phenomena sent by
something from beyond this world. Just as in economic
life man labours as if he were being supervised by
something other-worldly, so here one seems to perform
a task which pleases this other-worldly existence.

Reward and punishment, boom and slump, the daily
round and the extraordinary interruptions of it—all
seem to proceed from this irrational system. New and
incomprehensible inventions are made and they appear
suddenly like messages from another planet, resembling a reward bestowed by the heavenly powers.

Man has no wish to see the world of economics as
a whole; he has no wish to be its master, and not the
slightest wish to organize it as a planned economy
ensuring the correct distribution of what is produced.
He wants to have an uncontrollable economy, for
this uncontrollable character gives the system its
appearance of irrationality and makes it look as
though man were being punished by economic
crises as by a god. The man of the Flight experiences
within the economic system the crises he wishes to
avoid in relation to God. He would rather his soul
were shaken by the economic system than by God.
If he allows himself to be shaken to the depths by
God, the impulse of the shock will carry him to God;

and then nothing will remain but the individual man face to face with God. Not even the emotional shock will remain, for it was exhausted in the act of moving man towards God. The shock imparted by the economic system is, however, felt by man as a purely mechanical shock, flinging him from one thing to another, a fresh motive-power within the Flight.

There was once an attempt to connect one kind of economic system, capitalism, with one kind of religion, puritanism. Whether this connexion is a real one or not seems to us unimportant. What does seem to us important is that one should have been able to make this connexion. How loose and un-attached must this conception of religion be if it is possible so easily to connect it with economics. How mobile, how flexible, and how liable to connexions outside its proper sphere it must be, if one can so easily connect it with the distant sphere of economics. In the age of Faith it would have been impossible for the scholar to bring the religious and the economic into a partnership. The scholar would have seen that the religious sphere is absolute, remote from any relation of partnership, surrounded by a great gulf from which nothing alien can be taken.*

* We make an express declaration that no reproach to the great scholar Max Weber is intended. The reproach is addressed to an age for which we are all responsible.

LANGUAGE

LANGUAGE IN THE WORLD OF FAITH

1

JUST as God's Word is like God, so the word of man is like man; consequently it possesses body, soul and spirit.

The body of the word is formed by the vowels and consonants.

With the first uttered sound which begins to shape the naked body of a word, immediately there is born the entire space to be filled by the body of the word. Such is the enchantment proceeding from the first utterance of sound. The space of the word is ready before the body of the word and this space is also ready for the vowels and consonants so that they may build themselves up in tranquillity and safety. Also, the space is greater than the body of the word so that the word, when its utterance is completed, may have enough space in which to resound.

The soul of the word shapes the body of the word,

selecting the vowels and consonants and joining them together in such a way that the body of the word acquires a face; and this face comes to resemble the face of the thing denoted by the word. Certain words are the darlings of this word-soul, which has taken special pains over them, and one can plainly recognize the face of the thing in the face of the word. For example, in the word, *Baum* (tree), the *b*, which springs suddenly from the ground of the shut mouth through the small round of the lips, resembles the trunk of a tree thrusting itself through a round opening in the ground. Until the tree (like the *b* of the word) burst, a little surprisingly, out of the earth, the earth was everywhere sealed and shut. Then, there is a slight pause between the *b* and the *au;* the *au* does not immediately connect with the *b;* there is a slight gap, like a short interval of waiting in which one waits to watch the trunk of a tree growing upward. It grows quite straight; and only then comes the *au*, largely gathering itself round the summit of the trunk. The *au* embraces the trunk and fashions the tree-top which in its breadth resembles the diphthong *au*. But there still remains the *m*. With the *m* the mouth shuts once more, the tree-top acquires a definite shape which stands out quite distinctly; yet still in the *m* one catches the sound of the bees humming round the tree. Or there

I

is the word *Himmel* (Heaven or the heavens, or the sky). The mouth opens wide and, as it breathes the letter *h*, it aspires to the summit of the heavens. As one breathes the *h*, one's breath goes to the top-most heavens and there, where the *i* ascends like the song of the lark, there is an arch, a roof. And yet here, in these great heavens, dread takes hold of man, causing him to plunge into the depths of the *m*; and he hides himself in the darkness and undergrowth of the *mm*. But love, too, is there, as well as dread, and love suddenly descends from the heavens to man who lies in the darkness of the *mm*; and love calms and fondles him with the *el*. One might ask whether, in the same way, the birth of the word denoting the thing manifests itself in the French *arbre* and *ciel*. Our reply would be that in any language certain words are singled out from others. These are the darlings of language, shining out from the others, and their splendour enables one to see quite plainly their connexion with the things which they denote. These darlings are not distributed according to a single plan throughout all languages. That *Baum* and *Himmel* are singled out in German does not mean that *arbre* and *ciel* should be similarly favoured. The French language is favoured with other darlings in their place. Like Grace itself, the grace of a language chooses its own resting place.

The soul of the word performs over again the act of creation in the word. Because things have been created through the Word of God, the word of man is able to mimic this creation in the Word, and in the word the created matter becomes lighter and more buoyant. This process of becoming buoyant and lighter is dangerous, too, for the words might evaporate and float away altogether. But spirit is present. Spirit, as well as soul, is present in the body of the word and holds the soul of the word fast in the word's body. Spirit sees to it that the soul of the word gives form only to that in the word which has a real correspondence with the thing denoted by the word, and does this that the soul may not wander too far afield. Spirit is concerned for the truth of the word.

Thus the word goes out into three worlds: the world of the body, the world of the soul, the world of the spirit. From the three worlds power flows into the word, and this is why it is so full and round. It is supported by those worlds and this gives it its security in the world of Faith. The body of the word can vanish, it can vanish into silence; all the same, the word is not lost, for it is preserved in the depths of its soul until the spirit of the word shall once more call it back; and there, in the depths of the language, the soul of the word dwells, soul by soul in an inaudible community, ready, at the call of the spirit, to become visible in the body of the word. All words appear as messengers of that community dwelling in the depths, and this is why speech seems so rich. Only a few verbal messengers appear on the surface. For the most part, speech is hidden away; and yet the few messengers do all—and more than all—that is necessary. In this way speech has the appearance of ease and this too belongs to its perfection.

2

By the arrangement of the word under the hierarchy of body, soul, and spirit, the thought which enters the word in order to express itself is reminded that it must order itself under the categories of matter, soul, and spirit. First, the thought must relate itself to matter; there must be no thinking in a void. Secondly, thought must relate itself to the soul of man, for only thus can the soul of the word embrace the thought existing in the body of the word and lead the thought into the soul's depths and even at times transform the thought into something deeper than it was before its entry into the word. Thirdly, there must be spirit in the thought, and man must bring spirit into the word to indicate that all spirit proceeds from the Primal Word, the Logos, and belongs to it. That, too, which transcends the human order can be imparted to man in the word; for in clothing itself with body, soul, and spirit in the word, it has passed from that which is beyond the human order into another order and an order which belongs to man and is therefore intelligible to him. This passing of that which lies beyond the human order into speech, glorifies it; and when at times it proceeds as though taking part in a festival, this is not a piece of ostentation but resembles the wearing of a festal garment by one who, though humble in his own judgment, nevertheless is festive for the sake of one who is other and higher than he. God himself can reveal himself in the word, and so speech always seems greater than it is. As the Burning Bush blazed at the appearance of God within it, so speech would blaze if he spoke through it; the body of the word would be devoured in flame and the pure spirit of the word, God's truth, would stand out.

In the world of Faith men already keep their words close to God, as though they were trying to shorten his way into the world. Whenever two men speak with each other, he, the Eternal Listener, is there to overhear. But where the Eternal Listener is absent, all speech (even the dialogue) becomes a monologue.

3

The word is kept in place, not only through its own

articulation, but through that of the sentence to which it belongs. The word has its place in the hierarchy of the sentence. The order of things is as follows. The sentence begins with the subject, returning to it again and again, and again and again setting out from it. It is the guiding principle of the sentence, supervising it, plainly to be seen as it stands there like a tower, somewhat unapproachable. From there one can survey the entire sentence; and, just as round a tower there is a moat, so round the subject there is a caesura. The subject does not connect directly with the predicate. It is as though at the caesura it pondered for a little over what it should say about itself. At the subject there is a short pause for reflection, and a slight expectation on the part of the man who stands before it. Then, once the sentence is spoken, it seems that, though so much was possible, only this could have been spoken. The subject's power is so great that the uttered sentence can stand there as the sole possibility. Before the statement there is always uncertainty and expectancy, afterwards always certainty and happiness. That which is stated, the predicate, is really conferred in the way a title is conferred, and man is honoured in being permitted to confer the predicate on the subject. In the sentence: *Der Baum blüht* (the tree blossoms), how upstanding and complete is the subject *der Baum*. One sees only that which, in striving upwards, resembles the trunk. Then there is a slight caesura between *Baum* and *blüht*, and within it the tree's future, the coming of the blossom, is being made ready. This caesura corresponds to the short interval of night which must pass before the blossom can open. Now the tree truly blossoms. But when one comes to the *object* of the sentence in: *und trägt Früchte* (and bears fruit), one sees that across the predicate the tree is reaching through the branches, and the object which ends the sentence resembles the fruit at the ends of the branches; the growth of the sentence through the object resembles the growth of the tree through its fruit.

By no means every thought may enter into speech. The function of articulation is like that of a sieve; speech is not without its defences and does not allow absolutely anything to happen to it. The thought entering the sentence is not only compelled by verbal articulation to order itself within the body, soul, and spirit of the word; it is also compelled to arrange itself in accordance with the hierarchical order of the sentence to which the word belongs. Thought must reflect how to portion itself out within the articulation of the sentence. The form of the subject, rising like a tower, awaits the entry of the most important thing of all, the object of thought, which will enter, mount up, and stand out distinctly. In front of the tower the form of the predicate lies like a plain, spread out and ready for the subject to place upon it whatever it wishes: over the broad plain of the predicate everything lies exposed. Then comes the form of the object, a reminder that there must be a limit to the extension of this plain of the predicate, which must be marked out, enclosed, and fenced in. The rising of the object at the end of the predicate gives thought its limit, and from its tower the subject gazes across the plain of the predicate at the encircling hills of the frontier which mark its completion in the object. In this way thought is helped to model its own hierarchical order on the hierarchy of the sentence.

(Many philosophers of language argue that all feeling, knowing, and willing come to man through speech and that only through speech does he become human. We, however, do not believe he becomes human by allowing himself to be crammed full of whatever the language presses upon him. But rather he becomes human in virtue of his *selection* from what comes to him through language. He must, in relation to the language, come to a *decision*, and only through the decision does he become human, a moral being.)

Speech acquires rhythm by means of this articulation, and rhythm has a threefold character. One rhythm springs out of the movement from one word to another. But not only is there rhythm from word to word, there is also rhythm from word to silence, for after every word which forms a stage in the hierarchical order, there is a slight pause; and so a second rhythm takes shape, the rhythm from word to silence. But there is still a third rhythm, and this the most beautiful: rhythm from silence to silence. Words sway to this threefold rhythm and, heavy though they may be, they nevertheless move continually in the threefold rhythm.

As in the heavens the stars move in their courses, so do words within the arch of the language, an arch held up by things. Within it words can move with safety, and one feels that they move slowly in their courses so that, before reaching their end, they may once more reflect upon the end. The long path traced by sentences and periods resembles an ellipse, and within its curve the words fall heavily one against another, so that one imagines they will shatter one another to pieces the next moment. Then all at once they glide lightly past each other: at one and the same time language displays adventurousness and a sense of security. But at the centre of the arch of language, invisible, is the Primal Divine Word; and in the world of Faith the paths of the words describe a circle round the Primal Word.

"The corn was orient and immortal wheat, which never should be reaped, nor was ever sown. I thought it had stood from everlasting to everlasting. The dust and stones of the street were as precious as gold: the gates were at first the end of the world. The green trees when I saw them first through one of the gates transported and ravished me, their sweetness and unusual beauty made my heart to leap, and almost mad with ecstasy, they were such strange and wonderful things . . . Boys and girls tumbling in the street, and playing, were moving jewels. I knew not that they were born or should die; but all things abided eternally as they were in their proper places."

THOMAS TRAHERNE.*

Such is language in the world of Faith.

LANGUAGE IN THE WORLD OF THE FLIGHT

1

"Cityful passing away, other cityful coming,

---

* These two illustrative passages have, with Dr. Picard's consent, been substituted for the following passages in the original text:

Wie war dein Leben und Sterben so sanft und meerstille, du vergnügtes Schulmeisterlein Wuz! Der stille laue Himmel eines Nachsommers ging nicht mit Gewölk sondern mit Duft um dein Leben herum: deine Epochen waren das Schwanken und dein Sterben war das Umlegen einer Lilie, deren Blätter auf stehenden Blumen auseinander flattern—und schon ausser dem Grabe schliefest du sanft! (Jean Paul.)

passing away too: other coming on, passing on. Houses, lines of houses, streets, miles of pavements, piled-up bricks, stones. Changing hands. This owner, that. Landlord never dies they say. Other steps into his shoes when he gets notice to quit. They buy the place up with gold and still they have all the gold. Swindle in it somewhere. Piled up in cities, worn away age after age. Pyramids in sand. Built on bread and onions. Slaves. Chinese wall. Babylon. Big stones left. Round towers. Rest rubble, sprawling suburbs, jerrybuilt, Kerwan's mushroom houses, built of breeze. Shelter for the night.

No one is anything.

This is the very worst hour of the day. Vitality. Dull, gloomy: hate this hour. Feel as if I had been eaten and spewed."

JAMES JOYCE.*

Such is language in the world of the Flight.

This is the passage illustrating language in the world of Faith. The following passage, taken from an unspecified modern novel, illustrates language in the world of the Flight.

"Auftritt von der Platze, Generaladjutant, Lannas ihm schnell entgegen, die Altgott winkt den Dienern schon, wegzuräumen. Alle haben erfasst: Auftritt von der Platze, Majestät schon im Haus. Damen überstürzt noch vor die Spiegel. Erlauben Sie, lassen Sie doch mich 'ran, gnädige Frau!' Kennen wir, folgt Generaladjutanten auf dem Fuss, Herren Brust mit Orden raus, dalli ins erste Glied. Bedaure, Exzellenz. sehe jeder wo er bleibe."

Whenever in the language of the Flight one reads a sentence, it is as though one leaped across the debris of the word from one part to another, the parts separated by craters. It is no longer as in the world of Faith where the subject is like a pillar from which the sentence begins, passing through the predicate to the object, itself like a pillar. The pillar of the subject is cast down—in the syntax of the Flight one likes to substitute for the massive pillar of the subject some light pronoun; and though in the world of Faith, too, the subject may be replaced by a pronoun, this does not happen so frequently and then with hesitation, for here one feels there is something miraculous about one thing standing for another, the lesser for the greater—the pillar of the subject is cast down and so, too, is the pillar of the object, and both, along with the predicate, lie side by side, the whole a heap of ruins. The erect pillars would arrest the Flight, would stand like a barrier: but now everything lies horizontally, following the line of the Flight.

The articulation (of the sentence) into a subject linked to its object by the predicate is dissolved. The subject is no longer master of the sentence; each part of the sentence is equivalent to every other; the distinctions between subject, object and predicate are blurred; each word simultaneously resembles subject, predicate and object. The words do not form a unity;

it is as though with each word the sentence made a fresh start, as though each word had forgotten that there was a preceding word to which it had to conform itself, and a succeeding word, too; and so one word communicates nothing to another, at the end of a sentence one has discovered nothing that was not already stated at the beginning. Again, words do not approach one another of their own will; they are forced together. Nothing in the sentence plays a leading rôle; its contents fly in all directions, each word thrusting in a different direction; but towards what it is thrusting it does not know. In the sentence of the Flight there is an anarchy and, for this reason, thought does not grow with the growth of the sentence from subject to object, but is cast hither and thither, shattered into fragments. The thought which, in the sentence, seeks to unite itself with its order and, through its hierarchy, to unite itself with God, this thought is isolated in the anarchy of speech and becomes nothing but an isolated thing devoid of content. It is no longer thought; instead, there proceeds from the sentence something sad and lonely. Thought had entered the sentence with the intention of growing and of putting itself in order, but out of it there issues, sadly, something trivial and confused.

Since in the language of the Flight there is no articulation, speech becomes indistinct; one no longer knows where one word begins and another ends. Everything blends into one vast murmuring, existing before man has begun to speak and going on after he has ceased to speak. It is not so in the world of Faith, where the springing up of a word out of the silence is in itself an act; but here, in the language of the Flight, there is no longer an interval between the silence and the word; there is no longer the risk of the leap from silence into the word; both are dissolved in the murmuring. To make poetry is no longer to make the silence sound, but to reduce mere talk to a murmuring. One can hurl everything into this murmuring; everything comes to resemble it. In this language man can dare to express the most dangerous things, for in the murmuring they look just like the most innocent; the new resembles the old, all things have already been murmured in the distant past, everything becomes stale.

Within this murmuring, where one thing can no longer be distinguished from another, there is no longer the possibility of decision. Everything has already been decided, for everything is dissolved in the murmuring. But in the world of Faith that which constitutes the honour and dignity of speech is this: that in speech man makes his decision.

In the world of Faith speech is close to man; its warmth comes from its being close to man. The speech of the Flight is far removed from man, its very tones, so far removed from man, are cold; its designation as a means of communication, contrived for this special purpose, is a matter of pure chance. It is not so in the world of Faith, where speech can only be human speech, and where speech itself would create man, were he not already created; and this creation, too, is in the Word.

So it happens: the vast river of language springing from the Primal Word (though, unlike a river of water, this river is not narrowest at its source but is, in the Primal Word, at once at its broadest and at its clearest) flows between the ranks of men bringing them words, dropping into its silence, that silence through which time and again it flows, the impurities which fall from the men who form its banks. At times, in the case of one man, the river broadens into a lake; and this river of language plunges down into the depths of the lake, searching ever more deeply for its source, knowing that the river to be seen on the surface is not enough, that now and then language must tear its way towards its subterranean source in the Primal Word, so that the river may remain broad and deep and clear. In the world of the Flight this vast river of speech is broken up; its source is only visible in part; the former flood is no longer to be seen. Now speech moves with difficulty along short pipes and channels, no longer moving forward but shifting backwards and forwards; and in between are the parched and empty beds of the stream. Artificial waterfalls are scattered here and there, the words falling swiftly and, by mechanical means, being forced upward again in jets that they may sparkle as they fall once more. But this is of no avail. The water's language has a stale taste, whether it comes from the puddles in the isolated channels or from the artificially constructed waterfalls of words.

4

In the language belonging to the Flight, not only is the order of the sentence destroyed, but also the ordering of the individual word into body, soul and spirit. The word no longer has a soul and the body of the word no longer comes into existence by means of the soul but (through mere association of ideas) by means of the body of another word standing beside it. Yet in reality a word with a body but without a soul no longer has a body for the word to inhabit. It is nothing but a verbal machine, resembling in this the house of the world of the Flight, not really a house for man to dwell in, but a machine for living in. Whenever the body of the word dares to take the place of the soul, whenever it pretends that the soul

is not at all necessary—for body occupies every place—
then the empty phrase springs into existence. *God,
Eternity*. When these words are uttered in the world
of the Flight, only the body of the word is present,
and within it the vowels and consonants jar one
against another, as though the body were simply a
skeleton with the bones rattling one against another.

There is no longer a soul of the word. It has been
banished, for one dreads its depth; one is in dread
lest, if at any time in the world of the Flight the word
should be ill-used, it should draw down the body of
the word into its deep embrace. But while one is in
flight, one has no time to search for the word and
bring it out of the depths; everything must be ready
for use at any moment.

Since the word lacks its proper depth, it has no
place of waiting where it can be tranquil until the
moment comes when it must reveal itself. The words
hasten to show themselves—this is why the language
of the Flight lacks consolation, for there can only be
consolation where there is time to wait—and they
are all cast in one moment upon a heap, from which
one must swiftly pick out whatever one needs. One
body of the word lies beside another; they are no
longer separated by the interval of soul, and one
rubs against another. In this way, as they lie against
each other, they exhaust themselves. One word

x

diminishes through friction with the next word in the sentence. The final syllables are not yet quite rubbed off; but the final syllable only means something when, as in the language of Faith, something is taken from the tree of language and passed into the next word; where, as in the language of the Flight, nothing is imparted, flexibility has only the value of pure dynamism, the value of the Flight.

Since the word lacks depth, it does not ring truly; it has a kind of hardness, and, capable of outward expansion alone, it is exposed to every influence. This it finds disagreeable and so it takes on an aggressive tone, and, from the mouth of whoever is speaking, hurls itself at the person addressed with more violence than is intended. Always repellent, sentences of such words resemble iron railings or entanglements of barbed wire, and the individual words resemble iron rails with their spikes sticking up. The barbed-wire entanglement of language stands there like a threat, and everything entering it is foredoomed to be torn to pieces. Intervals between words are like pits for catching wolves: everything tumbles into them. This language gives no quarter.

In the word of the Flight spirit no longer exists. It is, in the world of the Flight, unnecessary to drive spirit out of the word, for spirit departed of itself at the moment man vanished from God's presence.

In the world of Faith spirit binds closely together the word and that which is named by the word. One could despatch the thing from the word back to the Creator, that it might be created differently, and the word would remain in its place until the thing returned and would then comprehend it as before. In the world of Faith one can put one's trust in the word. The spirit of man's word has a touch of the Divine Spirit who for the first time bound the thing to the word. In the world of Faith things press on towards the word, remembering their beginning when each one pressed towards the Word to be given its name. And even now, whenever a word cries out to a thing, one feels how the thing slips suddenly into the word and is comprehended by it. Only when the human spirit does not cut itself off from the Divine Spirit, only then has man's word enough power to keep hold of things. But in the world of the Flight one does not want the word to keep hold of the thing; everything has to be relaxed; word and thing have to flee, each one by itself. In this way the word is rendered capable of being commanded to go from one thing to another, as necessity requires. When the spirit is no longer bound to the word and so no longer has its place in the hierarchy, it must either atrophy in a state of dereliction or grow monstrously, and suddenly invade a man, giving him the spirit of levity.

5

In the language of the Flight a word is no more than a label loosely stuck on a thing, so loosely that it can readily be torn off. The label does not even tell us any more that a particular thing lies beneath it; it simply tells us of the presence of *something*. Now the word is only a means of signalling. At times vowels and consonants are no longer distinctly articulated but are contracted to make a single sound, a whistling. Whistling and signalling replace words in the world of the Flight. Though words still stand in rows, they are merely paths along which verbal signals may travel. If two ships wish to communicate with each other, little flags are hoisted on ropes: just so do words flutter up and down the sentences. When two men talk with each other by means of signals instead of using words, the distance between them is just as great as the distance between two ships: an entire ocean lies between them, the ocean of the Flight. And when, once in a while, someone in the world of the Flight succeeds in grasping a thing by means of a word, his grasp is so devoid of compassion and so triumphant that neither word nor thing can be seen; there is only the triumph.

In this world of the Flight where words flee by themselves, scarcely remembering their attachment to this particular man or thing, searching only for a

mouth—any mouth—out of which they may be
spoken, in this world of the Flight they sometimes
swoop down upon one who has no right to utter them.
Such a man then utters words that are exact and
good and lovely; but he himself fails to do the things
that are true and good and lovely; and yet, in spite
of this, the words themselves are valid; with this man
they have simply gone astray. In the Flight, where
the word wanders in flight detached from men and
things, one cannot be certain that in this situation it
has any value. And whenever, just once, the right
man has the right word, then he is in continual dread
lest the word should desert him. Those writers who
are (in the world of the Flight) judged to be good
worry over a word, wondering whether it will keep
the meaning they have assigned to it. In thus regarding
the word they resemble not a mother looking at her
child with love and confidence, but rather a governess
whose anxiety, nervousness and mistrust spring from
her profession. In the world of the Flight the poets
lose all their strength in patching together the bodies
of words as they fall apart and in placing one body
of a word beside another and in watching over it
lest it should slip away once more. How could anyone
still have strength enough to give soul and spirit to
the body of the word? In the world of Faith the word
has not only an intact body endowed with soul and

spirit, it also has a world to live in, the world, that
is, of Faith. The poet need not begin by creating
a world for the word; everything is ready, and the
poet can use all his strength in being a poet; and this
means letting the word strive with the world, that,
more clearly than the world itself, the word may
declare the name of the Creator.

Because the words, having been shed from the thing,
are scattered about and flutter everywhere, one can
gather them together and record them one by one
for the gramophone. Like something which is in the
way and is therefore placed in the lumber-room,
words are locked in the lumber-room of the gramophone, traced one after another in the grooves of
records, ready for use as soon as they are needed.
Now and then a gramophone record is played, not
because the words on it are needed but to verify
whether or not the words are still there, at least
whether they are still in the lumber-room of the
gramophone. Once upon a time the sailors passing
by the Echinades heard a voice cry out in lamentation:
"Great Pan is dead!" Just so one hears at times a
lamenting voice cry: "The Word is dead!" Men stop
for an instant and make a gramophone record of the
voice; in the gramophone it is no longer a lament but
a command: "Let the word be dead!" Men hear the
command and flee onward.

How is it possible for words which lie scattered and dismembered, more so than man himself, to become once again whole and living? Only through man's gathering them together and gathering them together in prayer and sending them to God slowly, and one after another. Man, in shame and dread, must become small; for the word which he received whole and perfect is returned in such a wretched condition that he must make himself small enough to hide behind the word; and so the poor word alone, and not he, will stand before God, before him who is himself the Word, the Whole, for only before him who is eternal and complete can the dead and dismembered be made whole once more.

THINGS IN THE WORLD
OF THE FLIGHT

WHEN the word is no longer united in harmony with the Primal Divine Word, its power declines and it becomes empty. But the thing which is denoted by the word can nevertheless continue to keep its true nature. Man is beguiled into thinking that the thing, too, is no longer there, simply because the word belonging to it is no longer there. For example, the terminology used to describe the Ego has to-day crumbled away and it seems that, along with the terminology, the Ego has itself crumbled away; and one actually says that there is no longer an Ego, that it has become lost. But the Ego is still there, in solitude, without the word. If it were not there, man could not even flee; even this would be impossible. It is buried beneath the soil of the soul, and the loneliness of many springs from their finding even their own Ego inaccessible. Such an Ego is, however, connected with another and similar Ego, and this man does not notice, and the connexion is transmitted by subterranean channels. Each solitary Ego is connected with all the others, and there are men of the Flight who are nothing but channels for this transmission; and this is all that is required in the world of the Flight: the Ego is handed on by underground ways, until the day when it forces its way once again to the surface, resembling a spring of water which appears fresh and is yet of ancient origin.

For the most part, however, a thing is destroyed when it loses its connexion with the word and (through the word) with the Primal Divine Word. Then the word loses the force which was transmitted from the word to the thing. (In the world of Faith the word not only names the thing, but also protects it.) It loses its power to keep the thing within bounds; the matter of the thing is no longer under control: it grows exuberantly, beyond all limits, anywhere; it becomes huge and misshapen like a monster. Man does not know that the thing grows and spreads only because it has escaped from the power of the word and can do no other; for him, to exist is to grow.

Take a factory, for instance. They grow continually, its smooth, flat, white walls which have no central point but are everywhere the same and are contrived as though for expansion; and they grow in all directions, smooth, flat, white, above the earth which has already stripped itself of grass for the growing walls. Within the factory, the walls of the rooms containing machinery do not resemble the ends of rooms but are like great doors leading into ever new rooms. But the machines, also, do not resemble machines for the production of goods; rather they are like those machines in the body of a ship which propel the ship onwards, for, in order that the factory may grow, they propel it ever onwards. The factory no longer seems to have been built in order that goods might come out of it, but in order that new factories might come out of it: it grows continually, and this is its sole importance. The production of goods is merely incidental and occurs whenever the factory stops growing for a moment.

This monster made up of buildings interspersed with railway lines and trains that it may move quickly, surrounded by much ground already devastated in advance, as though the monster had already lain down upon it, with a sky above in the midst of which an airplane appears, engaged in reconnoitring new country; this monster throughout which men are scattered to help the factory to grow, men who, when they move from one section of the factory to another, are like emigrants, arriving in a new section as though in a foreign land (so vast is the factory), men who die within it, summoned by that death dwelling in the factory who in his own peculiar fashion every week calls a certain number of men to himself, men who are not given up voluntarily but as sacrifices, that the monster may be free to grow—can this monster still be called a factory? No economic theory, no sociology, can explain this monster. It is simply matter that has freed itself from the word, and consequently also from the spirit which keeps matter in its place in the hierarchy of being.

Take, again, the high buildings of the city. The stones march forwards and upwards into the far distances and into the heights, stone beside stone marching onwards. The presence of man seems merely incidental and the stones tolerate only those men who quarry out for themselves square caves; the stones have no time in which to pay attention to men: they keep moving on, continually advancing, and, going forth from the high building as though from a fortress, are in process of occupying the whole of space.

And war, war which seizes everything on earth for itself and demands that things should become a part of itself—war, of which the universal presence is so

much a matter of course that it seems as though
war had been there first and men, the fighting fronts,
war material, only there afterwards, placed there as
points of support whence war may spread in all
directions—war, in which a child, looking at a
picture upon which there are painted a meadow, a
stream, and a fisherman, asks his mother: "Mother,
whereabouts in the picture is the war?"—this war, a
war after which peace could not be made because
so much war still remained that the entire peace was
pervaded by it—is this still war?

Then, economic crisis. In this men and goods are
annihilated and in such a degree that it seems as
though the crisis were not the consequence of
rationalization or unjust treaties between peoples or
incorrect economic systems. No, it seems rather as
though the economic crisis were created as a system
of economic annihilation (its presence is as much a
matter of course as the system of economic production), a contrivance for economic annihilation by
means of which economic goods destined for annihilation are produced so that the system may have
material it can annihilate; for the mechanism of
economic annihilation does not want to stand still, it
wants to work; and here, to work means to annihilate.
It is an economic crisis in which being out of work is
not the opposite of being in work; rather being out of

work is a permanent condition, a legitimate occupation into which one is born, as though the state
of being in work had never existed. This is no longer
an economic crisis!

So too with science. It also continues to grow
spontaneously, through sheer quantity of knowledge,
the divisions of which approach each other and are
mingled together, and out of this comes that which
is new, and this again mingles with the rest, yielding
a further increase in knowledge. This science has no
centre from which it grows; where the centre should
be there is only emptiness. Science is merely a rim,
and only from this rim does it continually grow.
Man no longer has anything to do with this science,
except to watch it and to write an account of the
mingling of knowledge and of its growth. Only
when it can no longer be viewed as a whole, and
this to such an extent that its growth is a tangled
confusion, does man go on to give it the support of
something resembling an idea; but this he does, not
that knowledge may terminate in the idea, but that
knowledge may continue to grow while using this
idea as a support. Now man is no more than an
employee of science; that science may grow, man
must do its will; no longer is he its master.

Phenomena only cease to grow when there is no
matter left or when a phenomenon has become so

monstrous that further growth would bring about its collapse. A phenomenon no longer orders itself according to the word but according to its matter. A phenomenon becomes great not as the weight of the word demands it, but rather as its merely physical equilibrium permits; it achieves a balance by means of its weight, and from this balancing comes the form.

It is as though the man of the Flight had deliberately made phenomena so monstrously big, that, set against the quantitative immensity of things, that which is qualitative seems, as it were, swallowed up. Things are only to exist quantitatively. While things determine each other quantitatively and quantitatively establish in each other an equilibrium and so put themselves in an order, they function of themselves and man need no longer concern himself with them. He can flee as he pleases.

So self-dependent are these monsters as they move, so utterly outside human influence, that it is as though they had been cast away upon an island in order that they might be quite by themselves and apart from man, as a kind of experiment to find out what happens when things become dependent upon themselves alone. Just so might one once have cast children upon an island to find out how, without adults, they would make themselves understood amongst each other.

But where is man while word and thing are being torn asunder? He does not occupy a position midway between them, for while word and thing are being torn asunder, there is nothing midway save an abyss. He has been cast off by the word and by the thing. Forsaken by the word, forsaken by the thing, he is prostrate in the abyss, that he may not disturb the fading of the word and the growth of the thing into a monster. He clamours and shouts in his efforts to create for himself a present moment between the word as it fades away and the thing which is about to become a monster.

These monsters, however, are still denoted by the words *factory*, *war*, *economic crisis*, and so on, though the things corresponding to these words are no longer there, since they have been replaced by monsters. But it does not matter that in the monster name and nature do not correspond. The discrepancy between the word and the thing even seems right, for the discrepancy operates to create an enormous tension. A thing of this kind, when it is summoned by the word, notices more than ever that it does not belong to the word and that it is entirely different from the word. It excites itself by means of the word and thrusts itself away from it; and the discrepancy functions like a motive-force, continually widening the difference between word and thing.

The monstrous character of many things makes them
nearly immovable (monsters are almost immovable)—
and they would become rigid were it not for the
vibrations created by this discrepancy. In the world
of Faith things live by the protection given to them
by the word; in the world of the Flight they live by
the absence of this protection.

This monster, composed of thousands of houses,
men, railways, odd scraps of earth and sky, finds it
suitable that it should still be called by the name
factory. When it hears the name *factory*, it feels all the
more that it is not a factory; it feels itself all the more
to be something entirely different which no one
knows, which no one gives a name to; and it can do
what it likes with itself. If the monster were called
by the name corresponding to it, it would not only
be recognized by its name, it would not only be made
tame, it would even disintegrate and vanish, just as a
monster vanishes when it is called by its right name.*

In this way language and that which it contains
are protected against whatever is monstrous forcing
a way for itself into language and laying it waste.
The monstrous things become ever more monstrous
by reason of the absence of the word: for the word of
man not only names things—it also protects them.

That other monster, made up of a riot of iron,

* i.e. in a fairy story (Tr.).

poison gas, epidemics, which is simply the rebellion
of matter against itself, finds it suitable that it should
still be denoted by the word *war*. It conceals itself
behind the word. The more violently it is called by
the name *war*, all the more violently it shows it is
not that which it is called; it hurls the iron ever
farther, the gases become ever more poisonous, the
epidemics ever more deadly and more obscure.
Defiantly it shows that it resembles, not war, but its
own self, the self of the monster.

These phenomena, these monsters having no like-
ness to things, make use of the discrepancy between
the words denoting them and their real nature,
keeping themselves in motion by reason of it, as with
a motor. That which is, in the world of the Flight,
still denoted by the name *marriage* (as though here,
too, human beings joined themselves together that
sex might be brought into God's presence), the
monster to which man and wife join themselves
simply to have somewhere whence they may rush
off in all directions—this monster, when it hears the
word *marriage* pronounced, makes man and wife
recoil from each other. The difference between the
meaning of the word *marriage* and the reality
resembles a steep gradient. A man begins to notice
that he ought to live in *marriage* only when the
confusion in which he lives is called *marriage*; but he

L

does not know what this life really is and all the time
he is wanting to know what it really is, he is making
the confusion still greater. Many a man who takes
pride in spinning round in this fashion could not even
do this, were it not that, on hearing the word *marriage*,
he notices he has been cast into this turmoil which is
at least *somewhere*.

These intellectual scraps, the pseudo-mythology,
pseudo-philosophy, pseudo-science of the world of
the Flight, would scatter and be blown away in all
directions, were they not denoted by the word *religion*.
But now, with this word *religion*, man—even the man
of the Flight—notices that these intellectual scraps
are not religion at all. He sees that they are precisely
the opposite, and, that he may know what they
really are, he makes the difference more and more
pronounced. A monster is born! Religion serves him
as a model for constructing a monster the exact
opposite of religion.

In the world of Faith, too, a phenomenon is often
different from the word denoting it. Marriage,
religion, as they are lived, do not often correspond
with the word. But here the phenomenon still belongs
to the word even though it may have fallen away
from the word. It could not even fall away if the
word from which it had disengaged itself did not
exist. The fall, too, still belongs to the word. But in

the world of the Flight the phenomenon that falls
away from the word makes itself independent, and
so great is its difference from the word, that it is as
though word and phenomenon had never belonged
to each other at all and as though no single thing had
ever had its origin in the word.

It is probable that things are even more monstrous
than our description of them, that their monstrosity
is so vast that human language is quite incapable of
describing it. Human language is not made to the
measure of this monstrosity.

A great dumbness, vast as the monsters themselves,
broods over things. In the absence of the word they
make great efforts to communicate by means of
sound; but the sound resembles in its uncouthness
the noises of the deaf and dumb. This dumbness is
so great that it could almost fall over backwards into
speech. But there is only the call of factory sirens,
rising and dying away, sending their call through the
whole world as though in an appeal for salvation
and redemption.

ART IN THE WORLD
OF THE FLIGHT

THE man of the Flight cannot bear the feeling that there is one thing and one thing only: the Flight. He needs something wholly other, something, now threatening, now friendly, which is above him, like a heaven beneath which he can make his journey.

The man of the Flight cannot bear the reality of the God who is wholly other, for in God's presence the link between one thing and another is severed and the only possible link is that between the thing and God; for everything comes to rest before him: the Flight is over. For this reason one does not desire God to be the wholly other, for God is a hindrance to the Flight. (In Dialectical Theology there has been an attempt to turn God into the wholly other in order to fit him into the Flight; but there is so much exaggeration in this, that all that remains of God is an "otherness" that is purely formal—his real

138

nature has been lost. Here the mechanical character of the idea of "otherness" has banished the Divine Nature.)

Man needs something "wholly other" which *helps* the Flight. This is Art, in particular the plastic arts. The very existence of Art in a sphere of its own already means that it is "wholly other", and from the beginning it is other than reality itself. The strange thing about Art is that a work of art is indeed made by man, but that once it is made it stands there independently of man. This gives it a semblance of otherness. Mysteriously Art has a connexion with man enabling it to be at once independent of him and connected with him. This is what man needs in the Flight: something having otherness and yet made by man and in consequence making upon him a demand no greater than that which he is ready to impose upon himself.

Nearly everything in Art is other than it is in the Flight. Here nothing flees, nothing is in a hurry; everything is tranquil, defined, classified, summarized. In a picture a fragment of the world stands firm. It is not as in the Flight, where every moment everything is changing. The frame is there as a kind of guarantee that one may quietly turn from the picture and allow oneself to be swept away by the Flight, and that on one's return the picture will still be there in its frame

just as it was before. There in the frame is a fragment
of the world. It was possible, then, for a fragment of
the world to stand still; and it still remains possible
to find a fragment of the world in its integrity within
a frame, while in the Flight the entire world appears
to be disintegrating. And so an all-embracing unity
still appears to be in existence; and to one who stands
in front of a picture, the disintegration of the Flight
seems illusion. Again and again one can return from
the destruction of the world of the Flight to a fragment of world which is still whole; and, as though in
expectation of our return, the picture is there.

The distortions into which Art has forced itself in
this world of the Flight are merely attempts to
render that which is alien and wholly other plainly
visible. Man has deliberately isolated Art in such a
way that its otherness is manifest. It is as though
those in flight had appointed a few men to fabricate
Art in caverns remote from the main road, and then,
all of a sudden (that they may give the impression
that Art springs from another world), to hold it high
above those who are in flight, as though it were a
light shining into the world of the Flight from another
world.

Even in terms of space, this Art is set in a place
apart, in museums resembling temples. It also suits
the man of the Flight that there is no general ad-

mittance to these temples, that only a few enter—
delegates, elect persons, who in the dark rooms treat
with Art on behalf of the others. The elect persons
then come out of these temples; they say nothing,
and this very failure to say anything makes the Art
within even more mysterious, and so there grows up
a still greater certainty that within there must be
something sublime with which one treats. Art is made
to appear something to which no direct access can
be had from the world of the Flight, something
devoid of all relationships. Then there is an artificially
constructed Absolute above man, who can flee all the
more frenziedly the more sure he is this Absolute—
like a god under whose protection one flees—is above
him.

The greater the difference between the various
artistic periods, the more it becomes evident to man
how rich this is, this *wholly other* existing above him.
At man's beginning it was already there in the caves
of the men of the Ice Age and in the wattle huts of
the lake-dwellers. The history of Art cannot sufficiently display the richness of Art and its extent; and
the man of the Flight employs the history of Art in
order to demonstrate the power and extent of that
Art which is, in its otherness, just what he needs.
The student of Art must labour for the glory of this
wholly other; the greater the glory, the greater the

security of the man of the Flight, who dwells beneath
it. This Art, wholly other as it is, is not terrifying,
rather, it gives glory to the Flight.

Whoever stands in front of the picture need have
no fear that he will lose his connexion with the
Flight. On the contrary, in the picture the world's
Flight is not annulled, it is simply concentrated; the
real Flight, far-wandering as it is, is condensed.
Such a picture is like a compendium of the Flight,
and this, too, gives it that appearance of being, as it
were, undissolved, condensed—just what it needs,
as we have shown. One stands in front of this frame,
waiting, until one finds oneself being thrust aside by
the dammed-up energy of the Flight, thrust aside
and hurled, as though by a released spring, into the
real Flight, and one rushes along all the more
frenziedly because now one knows that in these
pictures the Flight would still be preserved even
though one happened to forget it.

This Art is thus not essentially *other* than the Flight;
its *otherness* is purely formal, only an artificial *otherness*
which would be impossible without the Flight. This
Art can be manipulated from within the Flight and
arranged in accordance with one's needs in the
Flight.

Whether a picture is expressionistic or impressionistic, baroque or medieval, is of no importance. Each

picture is used by the man of the Flight to help him to make a greater and a safer Flight. A medieval picture is certainly more opposed to the Flight than an impressionistic one, for it is more complete in itself, more tranquil; but the man of the Flight does not perceive the enduringness of this completeness and this tranquillity. All he perceives in the completeness is the final expression before the departure; all he perceives in the tranquillity is the final pause before the Flight. He is glad to see in the picture the point from which he began, from which he launched himself into the Flight. For this man tranquillity is not the opposite of flight; it is only, as it were, the frozen Flight ready to thaw again at any moment.

The man of the Flight arranges all pictures according to the amount of external movement they represent. He sees them as though in a line, beginning with the early medieval picture which has that tranquillity which is for him no more than the Flight's beginning. Then, when perspective appears in the later pictures, he sees here only that things are becoming smaller, more distant, until they dissolve in their own flight; and so, too, in baroque pictures he sees only that objects are in motion, waiting until they can hurry away, but so far enclosed by solid pillars, for the road of the Flight is not yet made ready. In impressionist pictures all he sees is how the movement of the world is dammed-up in the pictures, because the world of the Flight is brimming over with movement; and he sees in the fragmented pictures of Impressionism only this: that things have not kept up with the Flight, that, shattered into fragments, they lie strewn along the road. For him all pictures are related one to another as though they were placed in single file along the line of the Flight: the line of historical development becomes for him the line of the Flight, the history of Art a story of the Flight. Only now does study of the history of Art acquire a meaning. He may perhaps make use of each phase of the history, for each phase can be brought forward as an instance of a phase in the Flight. Nothing more of much importance can happen to him, for by means of Art he has prepared himself for all the possibilities of the Flight. In Art, then, man keeps in store all the possibilities of the Flight. If all that happens in the world of the Flight can be rediscovered in an even more beautiful form in the world of Art, the Flight is made lawful.

Literature, too, is used as a form of that otherness needed by the man of the Flight. In literature this at least is true: that everything in it is cut off from life and this is enough to make poetry appear to be something distinctive at the side of the Flight.

In the world of the Flight, literature takes pains to be *other* than the Flight, for it is used only on account of its otherness. But at the same time it makes an effort not to terrify the men of the Flight but rather to pacify them by means of a purely external *otherness*. Literature wants to be something other than the Flight; but at the same time man is to rediscover the entire Flight within it.

In its functioning, literature resembles an independent mechanism: man can flee without troubling himself about it. Books spring into existence of themselves; one literary work produces another, as though without the help of man. The automatic character of the literary mechanism consists in this: that a work never makes explicit an appearance as a whole, but only a part of it; so that another work can always follow it, for there is still something for it to say. For example, naturalism in literature only seizes upon man's external situation, but it does this in such a demonstrative and exaggerated way that expressionism has to come along to show that the inner situation still exists. The deficiencies of literature are the mechanism by which it continues.

Such is the power which drives literature forward. It is not so in the world of Faith. There the poetic work is supreme and every trace of that which preceded the poem's coming into existence is cancelled out, so that man, in the presence of this supreme power, cannot think that there was ever another poem before this one or that after it another will come into existence. Through this uniqueness man is put in mind of his own uniqueness and this exists only by reason of God's uniqueness.

In the art and literature of the Flight, things are put out of shape, stunted, crushed, destroyed. One wants only to accustom oneself to the spectacle of annihilation, so one puts that which has been destroyed into the pictures and into literature. In fact, the world is already annihilated and there is no longer any need for God to destroy it. As if there were a race with the destruction ordained by God, the finish has been reached; and it is like a triumph: human destruction has won. It seems that God cannot catch up, for man is already far ahead of him in destruction. The destruction existing in these pictures and in this literature is more than exists in the world, just as there is more Flight than actually exists; and just in this excess, the world of pictures and of literature appears as though measured in accordance with the divine standard. This destruction—this extravagance of destruction—this state of being hacked into pieces, this prostration of things in pictures and in literature—all these are, as it were, *final*. It resembles a judgment in that for the man of the Flight it is a substitute for the finality of divine judgment. Once one has beheld the destruction of all things in pictures and in literature, one no longer fears a Last Judgment. One knows that everything that can happen has already happened. What God ought to destroy, man has himself destroyed.

THE IMAGE AND THE
FLIGHT

THIS must be said plainly: Only because man was created in the image of God, only because he is in this image, has he in any way the power to form for himself images of the world. God's power is not exhausted in his work; a trace of his image-making power is left in man, and this is what drives him on to make his own images.

In the images of Faith one feels the shyness with which the thing was put into the picture, a shyness springing from man's doing what in truth only God has a right to do, namely, to make an image. Only a few things are placed in the picture, as though man awaits a sign from him to whom belongs all making of images, a sign that consent has been given to man's presumption in making this picture of a thing. The picture is laid out on so broad a scale that God's glance may find thereon a place to rest. One feels its uniqueness; that is to say, one feels that this placing of a thing in a picture was not a matter of course, but rather that it required a special act, a decision. One places things in the picture with a certain precision, giving them a sharp outline so that, if they should not please the Creator, they may once again be jerked away. It is also possible to jerk away a picture belonging to the period of the Flight, but this abrupt movement belongs not to God but to the Flight. In the Flight things lack sharp outlines; everything can mingle with everything else, everything is being swept along; all things vanish together in the same Flight. Here the birth of a picture is no longer accompanied by a special act. A picture does not in any way spring out of the encounter between man and thing, but out of the encounter between an empty and a painted canvas. A picture was already there and out of it there springs another; the pictures beget themselves one after another, as though they had disengaged themselves from man and existed in a world of their own, linking themselves one to another and begetting new pictures.

Every created work which bears the trace of the divine power to make images has this significance: it moves, as one sees, into this world with reluctance; it longs to return to the place whence it came; one still sees in it the traces of the journey it made from

afar before its coming into the picture, and it seems
as though it had lost a great deal on the way, for
only a few things have completed the journey. If, for
example, in a medieval picture, the entire background
of gold, the golden walls standing behind the few men
in the picture, were not there, the men would turn
back. A little frightened, they stand in the foreground,
these saints—for those who first dared to appear in
human pictures were the saints. Often men have
placed a little dog beside the saints, as though to
advise the saints to let the little dog go in front, just
as one first sends an animal across a new and dangerous bridge in order to test it. These pictures stand
midway between a background, the primal image
whence they came, and a foreground, this earth.
The picture may not return to the Creator, to the
primal image, for it has to remain here upon earth
in order to remind one of the primal image; neither
may it come down again to the earth, for the things
within it were taken from the earth into the picture
that they might be closer to the primal image. It
really is intermediate between earth and the primal
image. Here is an independent region, that of Art,
and we believe that in this way a region has been
created between earthly and heavenly things, a
region which touches earthly and heavenly things
without these touching each other. So long as there

is such a region, that which is heavenly knows that
on the other side is the earthly, and that which is
earthly knows that on the other side there is the
heavenly.

These ancient pictures all strive towards the
original divine image; they possess a centripetal
energy. In the pictures of the Flight period, this is
not so; there everything thrusts towards the foreground, everything wants to get out of the picture
into the Flight. This centripetal energy in the ancient
pictures is that energy which wants to take everything
it has gathered together in the picture back to the
original divine energy.

It is easy for the picture to move back to the
original divine image, for everything in the picture is
ethereal (*schwebend*); that is, matter loses its weight
when it is in the picture, and this is so because God,
when he created man, touched matter and turned it
into an image, and this effect still lives on. Things,
too, feel that in the picture they move more easily to
God than is otherwise possible. When they are in the
picture, they do not press onwards; they do not fill
space so completely as they do outside; the Creator
can still place other things beside them, for room is
left for him, too; nor are things impatient, for they
know that every place is the same distance from
God.

M

For man the picture is a means of gaining control over things, for within it many things can be grouped together in a small space; and the man of the Flight can no longer control them because he no longer has enough strength for the true picture—as we shall see, the picture he makes is only a pseudo-picture. Where there is no picture, things, in vast disorder, lie thickly strewn, like brute matter, before man. There is no means whereby they can be lightened. We believe that the entire mechanism of the man of the Flight, the technical mechanism, is simply an attempt, with the help of a machine, to impart to things which are heavy, because they no longer have the properties of a picture, the lightness which, in the world of Faith, they enjoy by means of the picture. The whole technique is a race with the picture, a race to give things the same lightness as they have in the picture. We believe, too, that the picture will win, not the technique, for the picture has a reserve of strength from God.

The entire picture has been turned round to face the beginning, the place where once, for the first time, an image was created; and this centripetal force also affects those who hurry past the pictures, making them halt and guiding them back to the primal image. The picture before us is like a step upwards leading to the original Divine Image: and since the pictures are placed everywhere, everywhere there are steps leading to the Divine Image.

The man of the Flight will not tolerate them. He will not be held back by the picture; he will not allow himself to be turned round towards the Creator; he will not be reminded, or only as little as possible, that things can have the nature of images, for everything that has the nature of an image reminds him of the Primal Image.

The picture being created in the Flight is simply an abbreviation, a mere combination of things. That which in the art of the Flight appears as a picture is no more than a pseudo-picture. An image-like thing is being artificially produced by grouping things round some superficial and arresting feature. An artificial centre is set up round which one arranges things, for one knows that, grouped round a centre, they resemble a picture. This superficial centre takes the place of the Divine Centre upon which the ancient picture is centred. This centre can be changed, and now this arresting feature, now that, can serve as the centre, and it is a kind of game to think of all the things that can be placed in the centre. This, unlike the Divine Centre, does not hold men fast; it does not even keep hold of its own things, the things grouped round it. On the contrary, there is an urge away from this centre: a centrifugal force proceeds from these pictures out into the Flight. That part of the picture which indicates the centre is only a point of orientation for the things, that they may with safety find their way from this centre into the Flight. This, then, is the essential difference between the pictures of the Flight and those of Faith: in the former, things are centrifugally driven away from the picture as though they would flee still further away from the primal image, as though they had no feeling of security even in the imitation of a picture, as though in the imitation of a picture there was still a reminder of the original Divine Image from which they had fled. And this, too, is a distinguishing feature: that the pictures of the Flight lack the transforming power of those of Faith; instead, they themselves must endure being transformed, for the man in front of them may deal with them as he will. He is not bound to accept the picture as a whole, for the picture is no more than an aggregation of parts, and he can therefore fasten upon a single detail and give it the interpretation he needs for the purpose of his own flight. Things rush out of the pictures, but they would not have the strength to do this unless there had already existed in the world of Faith that power which held things together, a power which, in the world of the Flight, is trans-formed into a force tearing things apart. The Flight cannot sustain itself upon its own resources: even the Flight draws its life from the world of Faith.

Since man and things were created by God there is more within them than they need merely in order to exist. Where God creates an image, there comes into existence something over and above what is merely necessary. Things are alive in this super-abundance of being; they are not alive where all they have is that which is actually necessary. It is rather that they exhaust themselves in this actuality; but it is in this superabundance that they once again renew themselves, for it is inexhaustible. Because it (the superabundance) comes into existence where God has created an image, it continues to come into existence wherever an image is made. Every picture man makes is still hallowed by God's first image; it bears a trace derived from that original super-abundance and, so that it may become visible, man feels the impulse to give shape to things in a picture. In face of a picture he is reminded of God's super-abundance; the picture exists only for the sake of this superabundance.

This superabundance cannot be grasped intellectu-ally, or through a vague feeling, but only through love. Love is the counterpart of this superabundance. Image and love are bound up with each other. Love and superabundance face each other and in facing

each other melt into each other; but as both superabundance and love are inexhaustible, they continually face each other anew and continually melt
anew one into the other and thus nullify each other.
But the image is exalted into being the mediator
by means of which love and superabundance
meet.

We believe that God created man in his own
image that this superabundance might exist, that it
might exist in his own image and that for the sake
of this superabundance love came into being. For
it is only by love that the image can be understood;
for this reason man is the clearest and most intensive
image, that his image may call forth the most
ardent love. Of all faces, none has this quality
of an image to a greater degree than that of the
loving man—such a face becomes so completely an
image that its love becomes an existing reality.

Where love is, there is a stillness, for love is happy
to remain at its origin in the image: it clings to the
image. Love knows the image in detail, for the
details are safeguarded in love. When love vanishes,
the precision of the image vanishes too; and we
believe that this is why the clarity of the human face
declines in time of flight, for in this time love declines.
Only in love can the face be safeguarded.

Where an image exists, there is no past; the entire

past is worked into the present of the image, and so it is easy for love to forget what has gone before: it is dissolved in the present of the image.

When the image of a thing is destroyed, the thing is no longer able to persist in its integrity in the human memory; in man's soul it is no longer kept in its integrity; only the parts remain, stored up in his brain by the device of mnemonics, and it is easily lost. We believe that this is why men to-day so readily forget one another, for they no longer keep alive in each other the complete image; rather, there are only scattered fragments and not even all the fragments are there. Yes, in time of Flight, love declines, and it declines above all because it holds fast to things. This is what the man of the Flight will not have, this holding fast. And so the man of the Flight will not even tolerate the image, for the image engenders the love which holds fast. The world is being stripped of the image so that love's demand may no longer be made at all.

But perhaps it is primarily that love is lacking, and, just because it is lacking, that things themselves have lost their own distinctiveness. Perhaps, too, they are devoid of the image in such a monstrous degree that by reason of their wretchedness they may persuade love to manifest itself to them out of pity. But only that love which is highest of all can be summoned by that which is devoid of the image in so monstrous a degree: this can only be God's love.

The entire world of the Flight would already have fallen apart if God's love had not held it fast: God's love which has no need of the image in order to be free to love.

THE FACE OF MAN IN
THE FLIGHT

IN the face of the man of Faith, the individual parts, eyes, nose, mouth, are each created as though by a special act. Such is the perfection of each individual part, that it is as though for each a new creative act had been required; and each part is so perfect, so finished, that one does not anticipate a fresh perfection beginning where another ends. And though each part is exactly delimited, ruling its own appointed territory of the face as though it were a kind of realm, all the parts are nevertheless linked with each other in the communion of the Creator. The individual parts can be different because they are held together by and within this communion. In the face of the man of the Flight the parts are only linked with each other by and within the communion of the Flight; they are not created each one for itself but all together, simultaneously, as it were, by one single act of the Flight. The peculiarity in virtue of which each feature in the face of Faith stands out is obliterated. One part may very well still distinguish itself from another; an eye may very well continue to be different from a mouth. But each part is in itself no longer master: it is a bond-servant of the Flight and all the bond-servants of the Flight look alike.

The face of man can preserve itself as the image of God only when it is linked by faith with the original Divine Image in which it was created. As soon as man breaks his tie with God, the face loses the quality of the image: it falls apart. Those parts which, in the face of Faith, were held together within a unity which is over and above the sum of the parts, within the *image* of the face, are now related only externally, part lying beside part. Nose, mouth, brow, eye, cheek: each exists by itself; there is nothing over and above the sum of the parts; there is no image. The face of Faith is an image; the face of the Flight is simply the sum of its parts.

It is important that the face should be an image and not simply a grouping of parts. From the face which is an image a sovereign power radiates; it has not only compelled its own parts to come together within an image, it also compels the beholder to look at the parts, not separately and by themselves, but together as the image. Yet where there is no longer an image, only parts, the beholder is occupied now with this, now with that part; this one he can overlook, that one he can think important, just as it suits him. A man who deals in this arbitrary fashion with the face of another will deal in the same fashion with the whole man.

The individual parts, too, are not so clear as in the face of Faith. The face of the Flight must use up all its strength in keeping all its parts together, and not much is left over for the individual parts; the parts only hold together by means of the skin, no longer by means of the enchantment of the image, which, in the face of Faith, holds everything together without effort.

The face of the Flight has no centre, nothing within towards which it strives; it is not, as is the face of Faith, turned inward, centripetally, but rather it is moved centrifugally, fleeing outwards away from itself. The face is not, as in the world of Faith, a wall where that which is within ends and that which is without begins; it is not a wall marking the boundary between the within and the without; it is a purely external wall whence the Flight begins, a smooth surface from which everything rebounds. The face of the Flight has not, as has the face of Faith, everything behind it. Within, it is not complete, a *perfectum*, as is the face of Faith; everything lies before it in the outer world and all its parts rush outwards. It is as though the parts were engaged in a race with each other: the brow stands forsaken like the starting-line of a race, and then it too runs along with the others. The cheeks are like a smooth and vacant surface, for everything has already fled from them. The vacancy of the cheeks is characteristic of this face. It is impossible to imagine that there was ever a smooth surface which came into existence in any way other than by everything fleeing away from it. Each part rushes off (just as though it alone were permitted to do so), not caring what it drags along with it, not caring what happens to the parts left behind. The individual parts no longer stand in any relationship one to another; all that each knows of the others is that they are in flight.

All words have already fled out of the mouth in a fleeing face such as this; the mouth only repeats those words which have for long being lying in front of it. It tries in vain to give itself a sharp line: underneath it there is no depth of silence, nothing but a void; and it cannot close itself over a void. It gapes and stammers in the wake of the word that has fled from it: it gapes and shuts again like a mollusc. But in the world of Faith the mouth is finely drawn in silence; it is like a line, opening slowly with the word, expanding through it, and then contracting once again into its narrow line. Out of the mouth of Faith the word has a full sound, for it draws its resonance from the depth of silence. Out of the mouth of the Flight, it has a hard sound and it goes rattling through the void.

The eyes are, in the face of Faith, two rivers of light, radiating the message: "Here is man! Here is man!" This they do that created things may find their way back to man and, through him as mediator, to God. In the face of the Flight the eyes are no more than a pair of faint lamps, lamps which no longer glow for a single soul, only for themselves as they pass along the road of the Flight. In the Flight these are the last things, the rear-lights in the procession. And there is the brow. In the world of Faith this is a white ladder mounting up to the divine in the expectation that the divine will descend upon it. In the world of the Flight the brow has become nothing but a flat blind which waits for the face to become quite empty, so that it may come down and cover it— and that is the last of the face.

There is more in the picture of a believer's face than the lines on its surface betray. The picture of the face has depth. Between man's creation at the beginning of the world, and the image of man as he is now, lies his guilt. In his guilt lies his depth; and the more he feels his guilt, the more depth has the image of his essential humanity. The lines of the picture are like magical signs, signs of exorcism, standing above the hell within. How calm is the surface picture! The picture is the sign that God takes over the guilt when he pardons it. The picture of an animal lacks depth because the animal lacks guilt.

But when man flees from God and will no longer tolerate the sight of his guilt, then the face loses its depth; it becomes a mere blank. Where once there was the depth of guilt, now there is the blankness of dread, dread which rushes along no longer knowing why it is dread and which rushes aimlessly precisely because of this. Such a face, however, ceases to be a face: it becomes a grimace.

This face is contrived for one single purpose, that of the Flight. The eyes are there only to find the way in the Flight; the mouth wants simply to call out the signals of the Flight; the brow is like an angry wedge thrusting everything aside that there may be room for the Flight. Already the cheeks have been made vacant. The parts of the face are nothing but instruments of the Flight. In the face of Faith, each part has a specific purpose: the eye sees, the mouth cries out; but over and above this, the eye remains in the face as though it were not compelled to see, the mouth as though it were not compelled to cry out.

Over and above the fact that they have a purpose, they *exist*. What is primary is *existence*. The functioning of one part in the face of Faith does not proceed from its purpose: the eye is there not only to *see*—it is *there*, and so it also sees. In the world of Faith the face has more intensity of being than it has purpose. There is more being in each part, still more being in the whole, than can be accounted for by the purpose. The entire face, and yet again each part singly, lies within this superabundance of being. The eye in such a face sees, therefore, still more than the eye of the Flight: it not only takes something as it gazes, it also gives, in its gaze, something to the thing; it gives out of its superabundance. A human face lives upon this superabundance dwelling within it, and the things that are seen and summoned by it also live upon this superabundance.

The face of the Flight lacks this superabundance. (The face of the Flight has fled away from it, for it is the superabundance of God.) In it, there is only that amount of substance which is just enough to make up a face; with what there is in it, it just succeeds in being a face. For the face of Faith the limit is eternity, for the face of the Flight the limit is nothingness, and only in moving along the edge of nothingness does it still feel itself to be something and is it able to keep itself together as a face. The face of the Flight therefore lacks abundance; everything is scarce. There is no longer any breadth in it, for only where there is superabundance is there breadth. In the face of Faith, whenever one passes with a reflective gaze from mouth to brow and thence to the eye, it is as though one betook oneself from one part of the world to another. But in the face of the Flight everything is packed tightly, one thing beside another; this is what one needs in the Flight where everything has to be close together. Because there is a lack of superabundance, each part is bare, naked, exposed to everything. Unlike the face of Faith it is no longer sheltered within the superabundance. Where there is no superabundance, there also there is no reserve out of which the face can reconstitute itself whenever this may be necessary. There is also no space for the reception of the unexpected. The face of Faith is ready for the unexpected—which may be the Divine. In this face the lines are like roads of approach for the Divine, and they have their beginning prior to the face. This is what renders the face of Faith so great: in the whole face there is a kind of welcome. In the face of the Flight everything is disposed as for an attack; here there is one road only—that of the Flight.

The face of Faith is simply the centre—a visible centre—of a far greater face which is invisible. That which is visible is only a road whence it departs into the invisible. In the face of the Flight there is no more than appears on the surface; there is no road leading into the invisible, only a road to another face of the Flight.

The face of the Flight is a mere sketch. It is not made to last, only for putting up and then pulling down again with all speed: these faces are not houses, they are only tents. Men do not dwell in them, for they are merely lodgings. It is as though men put themselves into their faces only for the sake of talking, eating, and gazing. They speak, too, as out of a speaking-tube which they, so to speak, try out quickly in passing; and in this way too, they look out of their eyes—quickly and in passing. At times one sees a small notice hanging on the door of a house: *Back soon*. It is so with the faces. They are notices left hanging: *Back soon*. Alas, no one ever comes back.

Since abundance has greater importance than lack, variety greater importance than monotony, being greater importance than purpose; and since only in the world of Faith can man's face gain that which is important, while in the world of the Flight it appears impoverished and like something which has grown less, it should follow that man's face belongs to the world of Faith and not to that of the Flight. Only in the world of Faith can it preserve

N

itself; only there can it preserve those qualities that have been created for it. Even if there were no natural faith and no doctrine of Faith, one could still see by looking at a human face that man is destined for the world of Faith, not for the world of the Flight.

In the world of Faith there are also faces that flee. But here the flight is performed *within* the face. It begins within it and ends within it. In the world of the Flight, too, it begins within the face, but it ends somewhere outside it. In the world of Faith the fleeing faces are always related to a face that remains with God: in the world of the Flight a fleeing face is always related to another fleeing face. These faces have not fallen away from that which is higher and more enduring; they do not flee for *this* reason. From the first they flee just as though there had never been anything at all but the Flight. In the world of Faith a face can only flee because it has fallen away. It is from Faith that it thrusts itself off; and only thus can it give itself sufficient impetus for the fall. In the world of the Flight the face must bring about an inner disintegration of itself, that it may be able to fall away. This is why the face in the world of the Flight is so shattered. There is a further distinction between a fleeing face in the world of Faith and a fleeing face in the world of the Flight: in the world of Faith only one part of the face—and this only, as it were, after long consideration—is given over to devastation. One feels the obstruction, the resistance; but in the world of the Flight the entire face is all at once given over to devastation, as though by this abandonment of the face one could rescue something more important.

THE GREAT CITY AND NATURE IN THE FLIGHT

1

THE GREAT CITY

THE great city is the centre of the Flight. The streets resemble pipes into which men are sucked; and a few trees have been dragged along with the men into the city. These stand fearfully on the edge of the street. They no longer know their way back into the countryside and they try slowly to grow downward through the asphalt and to disappear.

The great city is the place of meeting for those who flee. They are in the great city by appointment, just as the gipsy tribes meet once a year at a certain place; and they are here to show that they all belong to one tribe, the tribe of the Flight.

They meet here to take lessons from one another for the Flight. He who is not yet fleeing learns how to do so here; and he who is already fleeing hurries on more swiftly.

Cafés, theatres, shops, are being erected; and while

in the front sections people still drink and watch and make their purchases, at the rear everything is already being pulled down and packed up ready for the next stage of the Flight.

When one looks down into the street from a building, it is as though one were looking down into a machine-shop: like the dark belting on machinery, the dark ribbons of men move backwards and forwards. The entire city is a piece of machinery producing nothing but the Flight.

Sometimes it is as though this Flight that one sees here were only something left over from a much greater Flight; and then the streets look like the channels left behind by its passage.

Again, people sit in the cafés and appear to do nothing but read newspapers and gossip. But each one regards his fellow with suspicion, wondering whether the other knows a quicker way of fleeing and hides his knowledge. All the time they watch the door to see whether that one is coming who will give the final signal for the final Flight.

Now men are like birds in autumn fluttering restlessly to and fro on the telegraph wires, still waiting for the last stray and for the one who will give them all the signal to flee.

The entire Flight seems to belong to him who gives the signal. He possesses it in place of a country:

he is king of the Flight. But when all at once two
gaze into each other's eyes, both know that each
is king of his own Flight, that the order to flee is
given by each one alone.

At night the lights of the houses resemble a loco-
motive's lamps, lighted for departure. At night the
houses stand with their lights just like thousands of
locomotives awaiting the signal to move off. Above
the city the moon slowly rises, sent by heaven (as
though heaven itself no longer found it worth while
to watch the city). As a spy in the heavenly service
the moon moves circumspectly over the city. And
the streets below are suddenly like traps or pits into
which the moon is about to fall. At times she seems
already fallen, the city's prisoner; and she shines in
the river far below and the moonlight is reflected
upwards, as though from out of a prison.

The great city is like the Flight turned into stone.
It may be that the Flight, having gazed down into
itself, has glimpsed its own face and in this way has
been turned into stone, as though its face were the
face of a Gorgon.

2

When from the fields one looks towards the city, it
seems to resemble a vast quarry torn from the earth

by an angry plough; it is as though someone were scheming to erect a building against the heavens; the houses are only so many reserves of stone piled up for this building.

The great city is built like a fortress against the heavens. Wherever the heavens are above, below on the earth there are the walls of the houses; everywhere city against heaven. It is only between the edges of the roofs that gaps remain: these are embrasures, look-out posts, from which to watch the enemy. The houses stick to the ground by means of asphalt lest they should sink into the earth when the heavens thrust against them. From roof to roof the wires stretch like barbed-wire entanglements. Now the streets are mere crevasses between the houses, emergency exits for those who flee. But in many places they are broad: these are ways of advance prepared for the attack against the heavens. And the factory chimneys are like the barrels of guns aimed at the heavens.

In the world of Faith the heavens above the city are friendly and near: they are the upper chamber of every house.

Just as there is an unseen means of communication between fortresses, so also there is a hidden link between the cities: the arc of the Flight stretching from one city to another; and it is as though the

great cities hurled men from one to another along the
arc of the Flight. There is no longer any land between
the fortress-cities: the entire land has become a road
leading to the cities.

It is otherwise with the heavens. Each morning
they pause a little on the horizon, considering
whether to advance over the earth's surface upon the
city and to crush it between the heavenly walls. But
then they swiftly rise, summoning up all their
strength to stretch their arc high over the city. There
stand the heavens up above; and below men look
upwards in dread lest the heavens should fall upon
those who flee, or lest the heavens should pull up
the earth at the horizon where heaven and earth
are joined together, with the result that everything
upon it would fall away: field, forest, city, and
men. The city would collapse as though the earth
had shrugged it off. For a moment the heavens pause
at their highest point; then they descend once more,
slowly at first, then faster and faster, towards the
earth, forming round the city an arc so wide that it is
as though the heavens had utterly forgotten that in
the day they stretched high about it.

Already the cathedral is prepared to gather
together all that belongs to it, that it may make all
safe before the battle between city and heaven breaks
out. It is as though the greater part of the cathedral

had already wandered away while the rest was held fast, though with difficulty, by the massive towers. Above, there is a tiny cloud, like a fragment of the heavens sent to meet the cathedral. A few houses have concealed themselves near the cathedral: they want to keep hold of it when the moment comes for it to thrust itself off from the earth. And there are animals and saints and children who have turned themselves into stone and put themselves into the cathedral that they may be rescued from the city. But there continue to be animals and children and saints within the city. They are already present as the advance guard of the new city which is to follow after this city of the Flight. Within the cathedral it is as though the entire city of the Flight had already vanished. Only the cathedral remains; and its arches do not come to an end where the building itself ends; they are invisibly prolonged to that other cathedral; and perhaps they draw within their arches the city of the Flight and by means of their stone turn it, too, into stone.

There are days when all men press towards the centre of the city; and they seem as though they had been repelled after having vainly attempted a sortie against the heavenly besieger of the city. Now the houses in their rows resemble beams hurled at the pursuer with the intention that he should stumble

upon them. But the streets are like trenches and the
men in them are the last troops covering the retreat,
while the others have long since fled. They are
noisy, these men in the trenches; they make a noise
in order to hoodwink the pursuer.

Dread of the heavenly onslaught is greatest at
night. Just as in the wilderness one kindles fires and
beats drums to scare the enemy, so at night the city
sees to it that it is everywhere illuminated and
that there is a great deal of noise. The green and blue
lights are signals, cries for help, help for the city
against the night attack of the heavens. Sometimes
it seems as though the heavenly onslaught has taken
place: the city lies there in the night as though it has
been repelled and hurled into the depths, as though
it has fallen into the depths of the sea. The houses
are like enormous ships broken apart and the lights
glide past like brilliant luminous fish; but the men
are only shadows cast upon the sea bottom from
above.

Even in the day the city sometimes looks as though
it had once, long ago, been battered into fragments
by the heavens, battered into fragments and buried
under the earth for many centuries and only recently
excavated. Just as beneath the ruins of Troy there
were still eight further layers of devastated cities, so
beneath this city there seem to lie in their many

layers the devastated cities of the Flight. (But in the air above there are already sketches of cities filled with men who do not yet exist but who will one day flee like these: they are the future cities of the Flight.) Men walk the streets as though in deep excavations between ruins. And the trees along the avenues are like those bushes which grow in the cracks of ruins; they are like an advance guard of the forest sent to occupy the empty city. Ever and again it springs up, this city of the Flight. Ever and again the heavens stand above it. They have now summoned all the stars and grouped them for an onslaught on the earth. Behold, what a multitude of stars already encircles the heavens! Then, when all have been gathered together, the heavens will hurl all the stars at once upon the earth. The stars will hinder those who hurry past in flight. O, that I might live to see this heavenly onslaught! O, that I might live to see ourselves so much captives of the stars that we should no longer hurry!

3

NATURE IN THE FLIGHT

The Flight has occupied the earth so completely that everything seems to belong to it.

The earth's surface serves now merely as the

ground upon which the Flight moves. This ground must stretch out far and wide that the Flight may have enough room to rush off in all directions.

Above the hills the forest stands black, as though something dark is being kept in readiness to descend upon those who flee. Everywhere there is this dark border to the Flight, the trees seem to char, to disintegrate in the Flight; and everywhere the darkness of the forest follows like a dark cloud.

The streets are no longer roads for men but lines of the Flight, white lines hurriedly traced, directions of the Flight.

The mountains stand like great pegs driven into the borders of the plain to secure the ground when the Flight rushes across it.

The heavens seem empty, as though everything in them had been swept away by the stream of the Flight which, as it passed beneath, tore from the heavens all that was suspended there, leaving only a few clouds to hide the cavities which are left.

Already the arc of heaven is higher, as though the heavens wished to save themselves from the Flight. But on the horizon, where the earth's surface seems to end, the heavens suddenly fall, close to the rim of the earth, and they fall so precipitously, so suddenly (as at a command), as though to hold back the Flight from rushing over and beyond earth's rim, where the

earth comes to an end and where the Flight comes
to an end on the surface of the earth. The heavens
are a limit set at the end of the Flight, no longer
heavenly in themselves, now no more than the
enclosing walls of the Flight.

At night, in the heavens which no longer belong to
the stars, but to the Flight, the stars tremble and are
restless; but they shine more brilliantly as though to
provide the light by which the true heavens may
find their way to the stars.

Already earthly things, age-old, grow restless:
Spring, Summer, Autumn, Winter, day and night.
With what gladness did the seasons once descend
upon the earth! How quietly did each await its time
to appear! Now the seasons of the year are restless:
as animals are restless on the eve of an earthquake,
so is all nature restless on the eve of the Flight.

Already the Spring hesitates to come. (How long
the Winter had to remain before it was allowed to
depart!) Then it comes suddenly, like one desiring
to make you forget his lateness, with greater violence
than in former years and fastening upon everything.
Now the occupation of the earth by the Spring is
like the occupation of a country by foreign troops.

All at once the Summer, too, has arrived, but it
is only a straggler following the Summer before, one
trying to recall what the earlier Summer was like

and walking on the heights of the earlier Summer as in a dream, shaking lest a voice should summon it to descend and even now ready to plunge into the abyss of the Flight.

Stronger and more clamorous is the red of the flowers in this summer, as though the flowers long to imprint their red upon the luminous air that this at least may remain after the flowers and the summer have faded into the Flight. Margins of the Flight flecked with red—such is the Summer of this time.

Autumn now comes only because the others have preceded it. It dares to take the risk because Spring and Summer have already done so.

The seasons of the year no longer keep faith with each other. Fragments of the Spring fling themselves into the Winter and Winter despatches a fragment of itself into the Summer. They all tumble simultaneously into the year, all together and one against another. No longer does one season trust another. As though on the eve of a great catastrophe, everything is dissolved, in dread, ready to speed away in the Flight.

THE PURSUER

WHAT dynamism there is in the system of the Flight, a dynamism so tremendous that it blasts itself and everything else into fragments! What an immense, purely mechanical force! What power to ruin and to bring to utter destruction is present within it—but how small is the ruin and the destruction compared with what might be, compared with the dynamism raging in the system of the Flight! It wants to ruin and to destroy—but it cannot do what it wills to do. For everywhere those in flight come up against God. He it is from whom they continually impel themselves into the Flight and he who comes from God, even though in flight, cannot ruin and destroy as he wills.

There are many things in the Flight, but everything which flees belongs to God. Those in flight could not even come together unless upon each one there was the seal of God's ownership. The entire system of the Flight would fall apart if it did not, even in the course of the Flight, belong to the one who is God. God's power holds it together.

Whithersoever they may flee, there is God. Wherever they find themselves, once more they flee away, for God is everywhere. Ever more desperately they flee; but God is already in every place, waiting for them to come. There is no place where God cannot be, therefore there is no place from which the Flight is absent. The Flight is great, for God is great.

Ever more desperately they fling themselves away, but they can only fling themselves so far, because they have torn themselves away from God. Only he who recoils from the stability of God can fling himself so far. Yet God's power is still manifested in man's tearing himself away from God. And only because God does not cease to go after those who have torn themselves away from him can they continue to flee on and on with such desperation. They are being hunted by God and they can move so swiftly only because he hunts them. Even this is God's love, that he, he and no other, wills to pursue the fleeing, so that he, the swiftest, may always be the nearest to those in flight. He not only goes after them; in the pursuit he anticipates them. They arrive and he is already there; in every place he is there before them. *They* follow after *him*. No one in the Flight knows the

Pursuer from the pursued. This, too, is God's love: he is so swift that those who flee are as those who follow—and this is the end of the Flight.

Perhaps the fleeing are gathered together only so that he, the Pursuer, can take them all at once into his grasp. A single grasp—and he takes them and not a particle of the Flight remains.

But the demoniacal factor lies in this: those in flight know that they can flee only because God pursues them, they dare to flee only because they flee from God and because God is swifter than they. They know that at any moment they can turn to God, that at any moment they can be with him; and therefore they run the risk of being absent from him at any one moment.

Always one has the Pursuer close at hand, always one can fling oneself back upon him and end the Flight. But perhaps one day God, he who is the Pursuer, may will to end it before those who are pursued. Perhaps one day he may stand still and pursue no longer. Those in flight, though, want to fling themselves farther and farther, but they cannot, for he no longer hunts them. Now he drives them round his own still centre. He is in the centre and they are in flight round him as the dead moons revolve about a living star. But as God is more living than any star, so are those who flee more dead than

any moon. What a spectacle: God at the centre and
round about him the dead moons of them that flee
ever drawn to him but knowing him no longer!
This, too, might be the end of the Flight.

But still men flee and still God, the Pursuer,
follows after them. Ever more plainly one sees only
God. The fleeing are simply coiled together like a
ball rolling before him. Everything that has obscured
him is torn away; the urgency of the Flight has
carried everything into its train. Never before was
God's existence so clear as now, for everything that
obscured God's clarity has been coiled up within the
Flight. One *wanted* to flee from him—now one *must*
flee. As if authorized by God, one drags everything
away from him into the Flight, everything doubtful
and uncertain that obscures him; sure and certain
God stands there. In the world of the Flight the
fleeing want to be lords; now they bear burdens and
set things in order, but in so doing they are the
bond-servants of God. They must help in order that
God may be seen plainly. Never again will a man
be able to say that he cannot believe in God's
existence, that God is a mere possibility; never again
will even one man call the possibility in evidence,
for all the possibilities are already held within the
Flight. Not one is left out; no one can concern himself
with them in private, for all of them have been in-

corporated within the system of the Flight. All that is possible is within the Flight. All that is real is without.

It is unnecessary to doubt when one thinks of God: all doubt is within the Flight. It is unnecessary to fall away from God; it is comic, like a copy—though a clumsy one—of the most monstrous apostasy contained within the Flight. The Flight is designed to be an enormous machine of doubt and apostasy; all doubt, all apostasy, all terror of God, are within the Flight, and one's own morsel of doubt, apostasy, terror, is being torn from one by the machinery of the Flight. Doubts, terrors, uncertainties, are no longer scattered, they are concentrated; one can no longer come across them upon Faith's path; they have been driven together and together they roll onward within the enormous machine of the Flight. There remains only God in his full radiance, his utter clarity; and over against him is the Flight into which all dimness and all ambiguity have been driven. The more the structure of the Flight expands and the more desperately it plunges onward, the more plainly stands before us the one who is alone: God.

The End